THOUGHTS FROM CASSANDRO

MICHAEL H. DAVISON

Dapa Publishing, LLC
Centennial, Colorado 80112
mhd539@msn.com

ISBN: 978-1-66783-693-5 (6 x 9 trade paperback)
ISBN: 978-1-66783-694-2 (eBook)

Printed in the United States of America

Dedicated in loving memory to Connie M. Salvatore (1941-2021)

Reality will eventually reassert itself, but not before decades of political upheaval have destroyed the nation of people who defied it.

I inhabit an infinitesimal speck of time between two eternities. Whether or not I make good use of this speck, I shall receive no other. *

*Expanded from a brief comment dropped by Ian McEwen into a conversation with Richard Dawkins.

Books by Michael H. Davison

Published:

Eshen, An American Colony, 2014, A science fiction adventure and love story, ISBN 978-0-9792437-8-3, available on Amazon

America's Suicide, Second Edition, 2019, An uncommon diagnosis of America's political malaise, ISBN 978-0-9792437-3-8, available on Amazon

Unpublished completed manuscripts:

Rahl, Advanced aliens visit Earth not to conquer or exchange pleasantries, but to plead and pay for help. Screened volunteers answer the call and encounter a civilization superior to ours by every possible measure of technology, morality, cultural amity, self-knowledge and happiness. After this mind-expanding experience the volunteers intend to beneficially change our world.

Lighthouse for a Shipwrecked Soul, A many-year psychoanalytical journey through my life, profoundly self-ignorant at the outset, profoundly self-knowing at the end.

TABLE OF CONTENTS

INTRODUCTION

I INVITE YOU TO JOIN ME in an exploration of ideas that transcend prevailing political and social arguments that – I will try to convince you – fail to come anywhere near the root cause of our interminable enmities.

A widely acknowledged principle affirms that the solution to a problem will forever elude the searcher until the problem has first been accurately defined. With our current political conflicts, we have not even achieved that essential first step, and therefore see political commentators propose remedies as bungling as medieval prescriptions for diseases the causes of which would not emerge for centuries.

This book presents a collection of rare or unique perspectives on ourselves and our world not found in liberal or conservative commentary. I urge my reader to reach beyond the tedious left versus right animosity and grasp a deeper understanding.

In his comic strip, *Pogo*, Walt Kelly once quipped, "We have met the enemy and he is us." Now let's see if I have put some substantial flesh on Mr. Kelly's accurate but skeletal observation.

ACT 1

ACT 1

Scene: An ornate room in Priam's palace wherein we find Cassandra alone, combing her golden hair.

Enter: Apollo

APOLLO: Fair daughter of Priam and Hecuba, I will have words with thee.

CASSANDRA: With me, my Lord? Your visitation brings unbounded honor. You, a god immortal, me a mere princess of Troy. With the woven threads of the Fates' decree must I within my living span briefly flower, then wither and die, the majestic affairs of gods unknown to me. My Lord, you mistake me for another.

APOLLO: No, fair princess, there can be no other. I have watched from high Olympus you, the fairest of the fair. The sparkle in your eyes would shame the exalted stars. The soft music of your voice would becalm the rage of Cerberus. Your smile would ignite a hero's valor who would face a thousand perils to win your approving glance. Your lightest touch would arouse a departed soul. As the angry red face of the moon glares out from within Earth's insulting shadow, so does the glorious flower of Troy eclipse the envious Helen. No, sweet nymph, I make no mistake.

CASSANDRA: My Lord, your wooing words would melt a maiden's heart. Whatever could you want from me?

APOLLO: Your innocent modesty serves only to further enflame my heart already bursting with love. No less than you I desire.

CASSANDRA: Scarcely can I refuse a god esteemed by all, my Lord. My amazement can find no boundary. Your praising words would win but for a hint of seduction.

APOLLO: 'Twas the first Olympian game, my sweet, destined to endure the vicissitudes of time and trump all intrigues of gods and men. My model, guide and inspiration, my father Zeus, who enjoys many a clandestine tryst to the unending wrath of His jealous Hera.

CASSANDRA: My Lord, you declare me a peccadillo, a grave offense for me, a fleeting fancy for you. What god speaks thus? Love's delights I earnestly wish to share, but not for shallow flatteries. You speak with a god's authority while deceitful raiment wear. Whatever might you offer for my submission?

APOLLO: You bargain with a god, fair nymph, a venture fraught with risk. Yet with reassuring intent this I will bestow: that you shall throughout your mortal span speak with the gift of prophesy. Never with a lie shall you taint the listening air.

CASSANDRA: Who could refuse such a celestial gift, my Lord, a value beyond estimate, praised by all, achieved by none.

APOLLO: Those words shall I take as assent?

CASSANDRA: Yes, my Lord. In exchange for your promise, I assent.

APOLLO: Gift to gift agreed, fair maid. At rising moon shall I return and share a raptured night.

Exit Apollo

ACT TWO

That evening - Enter Apollo into the same ornate room

APOLLO: Ah, my delectable morsel, the time for our tryst has come. To your chamber then.

CASSANDRA: Unforeseen strength have I gained from your gift, my Lord, and steeled my heart against a pact ill formed. What seemed wise to a guileless maid, better consideration has unbound. With the gift you graciously bestowed, deceit cannot pass my lips. I must demur.

APOLLO: Defying a god's desire incites disfavor, dear youth. My patience thins and struggles in vain with ire. Come now, and yield to divine wisdom far above your mortal ken.

CASSANDRA: Then I, my Lord, must disfavor over dishonor choose rather than yield to a passing fancy in a faithless bond.

APOLLO: Your perilous choice, my sprite, adds insult to injury. Of sacred honor you speak yet dishonor *me* whom you blame for *your* perfidy? Such I cannot dismiss.

CASSANDRA: An unfair contest you set on me, my Lord, a god against a mortal maiden untutored in the wiles of Olympian deities. This I must decline whatever peril the Fates decree.

APOLLO: Your final word?

CASSANDRA: Yes, my Lord.

APOLLO: A pledge made and seared with Olympian seal thereon a god cannot annul. Enjoy your gift, faithless coquet. To that I add another. I now depart and proclaim a curse to endure throughout the ages and fall on all Cassandras and Cassandros to come. Those who spurn the prevailing folly of their day, and with great courage and arduous labor manage to wrest a scrap of truth from the lair of ignorance will win no ears, only scoffs, scorn and threats from small but authoritative minds. This I so decree.

Exit Apollo

THE HIERARCHY OF AWARENESS

A N ATTEMPT TO PIN A SINGLE CAUSE on the political decline of the
United States would amount to a futile effort to simplify. Many causes
contribute and each of those rests on a more fundamental cause that invites
an ever-deepening probe laden with traps that if successful, would reach
down to some prime cause beyond our present cognitive and corrective
grasp, an unreachable truth.

Identifying that hierarchy of causes requires an inquiry into each of four
general categories of understanding that I call levels of cognitive influence:
the philosophical, the psychological, the presently unknown and the physiological (or inherent).

Picture the following blithe scene as a metaphor to illustrate our levels
of understanding of the political, social and personal problems with which
we grapple.

Imagine yourself among a group of friends and associates, one of whom is
hosting the group on his luxurious yacht. All frolic in the warm Pacific Ocean
under a clear cerulean summer sky around the nearly stationary boat that
drifts slowly with the breeze and current. Some of you swim happily about,
playfully flinging sea water on one another, while others float on personal
rubber rafts fitted with cup holders for wine, beer and other libations. In a
mildly inebriated atmosphere, all enjoy a lively conversation about current
world affairs, politics, philosophy, religion, the human condition and every
manner of belief from rational to silly about their God, government or them-

selves, and congenially poke fun at one another's viewpoints. Feet and hands occasionally dangle at the most about twelve inches deep in the tepid water.

Unknown to any of you except the yacht owner who is supposed to know where he is, the boat drifts leisurely on the warm calm water about 200 miles southwest of Guam. The Challenger Deep within the Mariana Trench lies directly below the yacht, 6.6 miles down, the deepest reach of any ocean on Earth.

The conversations are confined to the surface and visible level that we all see and argue about. Here the sun shines above the deep. This level encompasses science, philosophy, psychology, politics, religion, sociology and all the other topics taught and discussed in classrooms and that fill libraries.

No one suspects any unconscious motives in the discussions. This is the level at which the great majority of human beings imagine that they live and think, that this is all there is. Here various unquestioned ideologies equated to truth clash with one another, each heavily armed with filtered evidence and belligerent assertions impervious to contrary facts.

The strife at this conscious level derives from the primacy of personal beliefs, the universal obsession that has brought more sorrow and death than all the disease plagues of history. We can place at the feet of this perverse god all human-created woe. I can think of no exceptions. The believer's religion, political ideology, world view, doctrine, dogma or committed opinion reigns over all other considerations no matter how cogently argued or compelling the conflicting evidence. Since the believer presumes that truth is embodied in the belief, no further search is necessary.

We argue individual sovereignty versus collectivism, responsibility, dependency, entitlements, demagoguery, justice, left versus right, democrat or republican, conservative or liberal, religion or atheism, autocracy or anarchy, what's right, what's wrong, what's good, what's bad.

I suggest that the fundamental attitude underlying the arguments at this surface level is each person's imagined balance between a presumption that he or she has chosen his or her own ethical standards, course of life and obligations to self, loved ones and society; versus standards and obligations imposed on the individual by external authorities that the individual rejects. That balance point differs for each person. People living at this surface level of consciousness imagine themselves guided by reasoning, feelings and pragmatism. And they are mistaken.

Then we go deeper.

Further down we find increasingly darker, colder, less explored depths that sunlight still reaches but with ever decreasing illumination with increasing depth. Here is the psychological stratum wherein operates our mostly unconscious predilections, passions, envies, fears and unexamined beliefs and attitudes about self and others.

This stratum is profoundly influenced by early familial, cultural and circumstantial forces that etch a unique collection of refractory marks on each individual. Here is the domain of the psychiatrists and clinical psychologists who probe the murky depths of their patients' minds to coax bits of insight into the light. Often with disheartening results over lengthy periods of time, they grapple with neurosis, psychosis, demented minds, mis-understood and mis-directed hatred and rage (like Hitler and the Jews), depression, narcissism, bipolar disorder (manic depression), poor self-awareness and traumatized children who grew up as enraged adults but failed to identify the real reason for their rage, all occasionally illuminated by insights that expose reality.

Most of us live unaware or uncaring about the unconscious influences that urge us toward beliefs ranging from the profound to the absurd. Animating this level of non-awareness is a persistent but disguised yearning to regress to a child's dependence on, and want of, a loving, indulgent, devoted mommy and a protecting, guiding, infallible daddy. We are, *all of us*, grown up children.

We do not know ourselves at all well and are partially but powerfully driven by unconscious mental processes. We do not know why we love, hate and pursue some end rather than another, and persist in assigning the wrong causes to our emotions or choices especially if the real cause is embarrassing, frightening or anguishing. We much prefer to believe what feels good and reassuring over what is true.

Then we go deeper.

Below the unconscious level lurk realities within our capacity to understand and that profoundly affect us but operate beyond our present knowledge. Harmful natural phenomena were once given supernatural explanations. A good example from the past is the unknown existence of microorganisms prior to the invention of the microscope. Our ancestors had not a clue what caused the diseases that decimated and terrified them. A human body hosts trillions of bacteria and other microbes without which we could not live but rarely, if ever, think about. They are literally the foundation of life, yet humans were oblivious to their presence for the greatest part of our history.

Before the age of enlightenment, interpretations of devastating storms, fires, floods, earthquakes and famines terrified people who had no idea of their causes and blamed punitive gods or suspicious people in league with demons.

Then we go deeper.

Next down, the bottom stratum, the cold, lightless and undisturbed depths I label the intrinsic, inherent or physiological. Here operate our individual genetic endowments and anatomical and cognitive limitations over which we have no control. This level can best be elucidated with a question: what truths about ourselves, the universe and our place in it are not only beyond our present understanding but *beyond our capacity to understand* in the same manner as algebra lies far beyond the grasp of a chimpanzee? The mental capacity is not there. A friend once pictured this as a dog in a library. The English scientist, J.B.S. Haldane (1892-1964), probably expressed it best, "My own suspicion is that the universe is not only queerer than we suppose, but queerer than we can suppose." No degree of introspection can reveal the forces that affect us at this level.

We see examples all around us in most people's inability to grasp advanced mathematics or the latest confirmations of relativity and quantum mechanics. Human cognition expresses itself over a wide range with an Einstein at the top and the guy who can't find the bathroom anchoring the bottom. Einstein's mind was as far above the lowest levels of human intellectual strata as those levels function above that of a chimp.

Down here all is lightless, cold and utterly indifferent to our survival. This is the ontological tap root, the base, the bottom of where we now find ourselves. We can't probe any deeper until we have the mental capacity to do so. Here the Challenger Deep metaphor fails us. Still greater depths await us in some distant future, depths beyond our present capacity to even imagine much less grasp.

Each of these hierarchic levels without doubt influences, in varying degrees, our beliefs, thoughts, emotions, behavior and choices.

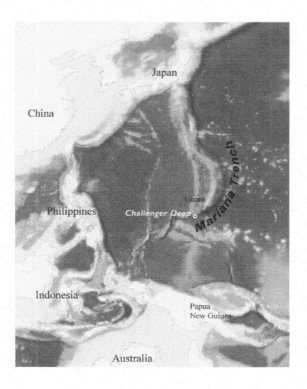

REFUSING TO SEE THE ELEPHANT
IN THE LIVING ROOM

W HEN THE APPLICATION OF A PUBLIC POLICY consistently produces
outcomes not only opposite those promised by its proponents but
actually brings great harm to the infected polity, reason demands that we at
least question the honesty of the proponent's stated motives. That consideration leads to the disturbing possibility that the salubrity promised by the
proponents of an ill-fated idea was a subterfuge designed to disguise the truth
that the harmful results were the originally intended ones.

That line of inquiry logically leads to the question, why would any
group deliberately advocate policies that have unfailingly led to widespread
economic decline and moral degeneration? Three possible explanations
come to mind:

1. Many people do not look too deeply into the causes of our decline, or
   do not even acknowledge that we are sliding down a slippery slope.
   They see a society that permits great disparities in wealth, talent and
   accomplishment as unjust and must be "corrected" with egalitarian distribution schemes and replaced with a "fairer" system, both
   accomplished through democratic voting. I think that these people
   hold an erroneous concept of justice promulgated by popular sources
   of information and indoctrinated by our educational system. Nor do

they see the psychopaths (future Lenins, Stalins, Hitlers and Maos) manipulating the decline from off stage. More in later chapters.

2. Promoters of the deleterious idea strive to bankrupt and otherwise bring to ruin a political structure they see as unjust so that they can supplant it with their statist ideal, for example, the partisans of Saul Alinsky (1909-1972) who advised his readers to never let a crisis go to waste as long as it advances the statist specter. That the many previous political applications of these identical ideals have never failed to bring disaster does not deter them, an observation that brands them as monumentally stupid, evil or both.

3. Using the personalities and actions of Lenin, Stalin, Hitler and Mao as examples, proponents of politically lethal ideas burn with a psychopathological passion to impart onto the rest of humanity the rage and hatred engendered in their very early life experience and the deranged mental outlook derived from it.

Fully convinced that their theistic or political doctrine is correct and must prevail over all of humanity, doctrinaires rationalize every conceivable action spanning the range from honorable to genocidal to bring about the global triumph of their belief. Lies cease to be lies and killing any number among the uncooperative escapes the heinous stamp of murder. In accordance with their perverse logic, they rationalize lies, deceit and genocide under the pretense of pursuing a "higher" cause of social justice that instead inevitably delivers a dystopia of dependency, irresponsibility, entitlement, demagoguery, gobs of intrusive government and social IN-justice.

The travesty continuously reenacts the hackneyed drama of asserting the desired conclusion *first*, ahead of any refuting evidence: "My belief is true to the last jot and must prevail over all of humanity. Those who stand in the way must be destroyed." In other words, the doctrine, whatever it might be, is axiomatic, beyond argument. Advocates then pledge themselves to reify that belief no matter the cost in blood, death, treasure and tears.

An immediate solution to our political conflicts does not exist even as an imagined ideal. But working toward an amelioration will first require removal of the chief obstacle to the progress of rational thought. We must first abandon our desperate clinging to beliefs, here defined as adherence to a set of related ideas that comprise an unquestioned and defended doctrine equated to truth that tolerates no opposition, one accepted with no respect for *real* truth as opposed to an emotional commitment to a cherished view, one that automatically trumps all evidence and all arguments. Entrenched unquestioned beliefs comprise the root of societal conflict, decline and war. Most disastrously the prevailing conviction is that the other guy's beliefs are in error. Mine are correct. The dogmatists declare, "Our ideology is true. We interpret reality accordingly and will force you to conform to it."

So, what is the nature of the Elephant in the Living Room, the sickness that afflicts the world, the tap root of all human-caused woe? Some thoughts on the question:

1. Human evolution has reached nowhere near the point when our self-understanding can even be considered adequate let alone good. Consequently, we have only the vaguest understanding of why we believe and behave as we do. We rationalize spurious explanations for those beliefs and behaviors that exonerate, flatter us or feel good, then accept those rationalizations as true.

2. We look for answers in the wrong places. This brings to mind the old joke about looking for the lost wallet under the lamp post because that's where the light shines. But it is not where the wallet will be found. To make matters worse, the wallet hides submerged in a murky mud puddle, so it remains hidden even in daylight hours.

3. The numerous theistic and political religions to which humans have always clung for understanding of self and reality have proven to be gigantic delusions and cannot serve as viable standards of morality. A majority of people now deplorably derive their moral standards

from welfare statist premises, themselves full of error and dogmatic certainties.

4. We presently rush headlong on a course that can only lead to unprecedented catastrophe mainly brought on by #3.

5. The principal pernicious beliefs presently driving us toward disaster can be identified as feelings of resentment, envy and helplessness toward those who accomplish or pull the strings of power. Those presumptions in collusion with pandering demagogues foster convictions of entitlement, moral degeneration and universal larceny.

6. The perennial appeal of theistic and political beliefs grows out from the near universal yearning to mitigate the brutal realities of living: disease, pain, losses, grief, disappointments, failings, adversities of man and Nature, envy of those better off, the brevity of life and uncertainties about what is true and right. These outweigh the ephemeral joys and contentment that we manage to create.

7. Only a very difficult and painfully honest *individual* look inward at one's own theistic and political beliefs (religions) and what they do to us individually and collectively has any chance of arresting much less reversing our plunge toward catastrophe. Each of us must face a lifelong pursuit of what is *really* true, a quest that can have no end, not strive to impose our version of it on everybody else.

So, the metaphors of the elephant, the lost wallet, the lamp post, the light under it, and the mud puddle refer to what?

We are looking for the answers to our political and social conflicts and remedies for personal misfortunes in the wrong places. We anguish over who will win, republican or democrat, liberal or conservative, the right or the left, and blame that other political party for our social and political woe. We invent superficial answers and ill-fated remedies that to us seem right and just, illuminated by that small part of reality that we imagine we see clearly (searching in the light under the lamp post). But the invented answers are neither right nor just. Valuable answers will only be found hidden in the unconscious recesses of our minds (the wallet full of money submerged in the mud puddle- our cognitive muddle). Our common refusal to see our social and political conflicts as individually psychological and to examine the denied influences that lie within each of us (the elephant in the living room of our mind) dooms our search for realistic answers. Too many people resist the thought of self-examination with feelings from indifference to repugnance, a range that includes fear, contempt and dismissal as an unnecessary waste of time promoted by frauds.

I often wonder if most people are so committed to their beliefs as to be incapable of searching for and finding truth. To answer the question *what is true* first requires allegiance to the imperfect but only means we have to discover it, the methodology of science. We must search for the wallet not only in the dark away from the lamp post, but in the cognitive mud puddle of our confusion and uncertainty.

We have cause to wish that our better thinkers would draw on their wisdom to transcend our petty political squabbles that have no hope of touching the root of the human condition that we all must endure.

It is frustrating for me to so often observe people who call themselves conservatives fail to grasp the nature and extent of the evil they face. They grapple with the enemy in minor skirmishes with obsolete weapons as if afraid to engage the opposing armies in the principal theater of conflict, the fog enshrouded field of psychological understanding. What we face today cannot be understood in terms of religion, philosophy or political commentary, but looms like a specter arising from a morass of psychopathology.

Conservatives collaborate with leftist deceit when they describe their opponents as "liberals," "progressives" or "well meaning." Could and can Fidel Castro, Hugo Chavez, Bernie Sanders or Jeremy Corbyn be honestly described as well meaning? These people were and are not stupid. They could see the past and present sanguinary catastrophes brought about by the political applications of their ideas. If you decline to label them evil, to me a much-deserved adjective, then at least consider the possibility that they were and are mentally sick.

We cannot understand the etiology of a deranged personality without examining that individual's genetic endowment and childhood experiences. Most often such a study is usually dismissed as irrelevant or accomplished poorly or scurrilously if at all. Nevertheless, those are the only inquiries where the truth has any chance to surface.

Citing a well known example from the 20th Century's most horrifying catastrophe, WWII, and looking only in the light under the lamp post, we would conclude that Hitler's notoriously focused rage resulted in the murders of six and a half million Jews and many millions of others. But was he fundamentally enraged at Jews despite his many affirming vituperations, or seeking an outlet for hatred and revenge against substitute offenders while the real offenses had wrought their psychic damage long before in some perverse and denied childhood experiences?

Those very early offenses were consciously "forgotten," but he imparted the resulting rage, still violent and demanding resolution, with adult force and a delusional focus, his outward malice a projection of hatred forged during an early abusive life that he could not face. Sourcing Hitler's virulent hatred in his adverse childhood makes much more sense than presuming he acquired it by immersing himself in anti-Semitic authors and exaggerated Jewish economic influence.

Anyone denying his own source of explosive rage can easily find vulnerable scapegoats in some defenseless group. Clearly this is yet another psychoanalytic speculation in an attempt to explain a deranged personality that brought so much sorrow to a world already surfeit with sorrows. But how else are we to understand such people? In any case we must not assume that understanding implies exoneration. We remain everywhere and always responsible for what we think and do even though we might not know why.

We cannot crawl inside people's minds and see what seethes therein. Nevertheless, as difficult or impossible that such probing might be, the answers about ourselves and others that we so desperately seek are to be found nowhere else. Failing to find truth in the light under the lamp post forces the search elsewhere and that means within the mind. Only there will we find the roots of our torments and terrors that have sprouted into hatreds and conflicts that manifest themselves in the world's human-caused horrors.

Before my final sunset I would love to see at least a small ray of enlightenment stab the specter of hateful violent conflict that has brutalized this world over my entire lifetime.

I was born at a time when Hitler and Tojo menaced the world. With their malice defeated at grievous cost to everyone, a potentially worse one rose like a miasma out of Russia. Then China had to affirm its despotic arrogance and parade its missiles. Then Muslim fanatics murdered and destroyed in the name of their invented god.

Now, potentially worst of all, the ancient ugly face of statism masquerading as liberal, progressive and compassionate looms over the country of my birth, the country that has given the world so much and promises still more, the country I love.

When will enough people finally get into their heads the ideas that:

1. Our enemy agitates with differing levels of influence within each of us, encapsulated in the convictions that our fanciful and conflicting beliefs must be belligerently defended against all assaults because they bring to each of us an assuring but deceptive grasp of reality.
2. The entire leftist agenda with its hypocrisy, pretenses and self-flatteries is a gigantic and ominous fraud.
3. We refuse to see the elephant in the living room.

We anguish over who will win, republican or democrat, liberal or conservative, the right or the left. Surely our better thinkers have the wisdom to transcend these petty squabbles that have no hope of touching the root of the human condition that we all must endure.

We all yearn to breathe free but carry chains inside our heads. Those chains hold people in bondage unless and until they recognize and identify the nature of their internal chains and with rare determination and difficult effort cast them off. Chains take the form of beliefs, that is, doctrines held to be true but unsupported by evidential reality.

I leave readers with an appeal: stop collaborating with political types who cloak themselves in deceitful self-flatteries like liberal, progressive, freedom-loving, well-meaning and compassionate, or collude with their hypocritical cries for social justice. What they really want has nothing to do with any concept of justice, social or otherwise. The evidence strongly points away from probity and toward clandestine and sinister intentions that have been sanitized as a campaign for justice.

THE LEFT-RIGHT SNARE

Excerpt from *America's Suicide*, 2nd Edition

F ORCED AT LAST to reluctantly concede to demands for a representative assembly, Louis XVI of France in his regulations of January 24, 1789, for the convocation of the Estates General, decreed, among many other things, that "In sessions the order of the Clergy shall sit on the right, the order of the nobility on the left, and that of the third estate opposite."[1] The Estates General was thus assembled for the first time since 1614 on May 5, 1789.

Representatives of the third estate, the aristocrats' term for the common working people, understandably displeased with both the seating arrangement and the subsequent impotence of the Estates General, assembled on a tennis court on June 17, 1789, with some of their members and a few lesser clergymen, and swore an oath to form a body of the common people separate from the Estates General. They declared that body the National Assembly.[2] This group would later evolve into the Revolutionary Legislative Assembly (October 1, 1791 to September 20, 1792) in which the 745 members seated themselves generally in accordance with their attitudes toward the monarchy. On the right approximately 250 conservatives supported a constitutional monarchy, particularly stressing fiscal reform but opposed to major upheavals of the existing political structure. To them a king was acceptable provided that constitutional law limited his powers and held him accountable for his actions. On the left sat 150 radicals supported principally by the Jacobin and Cordelier clubs who distrusted monarchy and worked to establish democracy. In the center floated the moderates with "no definite policies, [who] voted now with the Right, now with the Left, as circumstances dictated."[3]

French historian Maurice Duverger, writing about early nineteenth century France, places those loyal to the republic on the left and "its enemies, Bonapartists, Orleanists, Legitimists, and supporters of dictatorship" on the right.[4] He then suggests that the left-right dichotomy later assumed its modern sense with the introduction of the element of socialism. His use in the following quotation of the term *liberal* refers to the classic liberal who was an advocate of free markets and limited government, and not to the contemporary American understanding of that word:

> Toward the end of the nineteenth century the traditional cleavages between liberal and conservative, republican and antirepublican, clerical and anticlerical, were disrupted by the question of socialism. Many liberals, republicans, and anticlericals were still attached to private ownership of the means of production and to economic competition; hence they were antiSocialist. On this issue they joined forces with the traditional conservatives in an antiSocialist coalition. Consequently, from this point of view the Right could be defined as upholding liberal capitalism and private enterprise, while the Left would be composed of those who desired the coming of a Socialist system or at least state control of the production of wealth and egalitarian distribution of the national income. Obviously, there exist intermediate positions. To support the extension of social security, state control of investments, the intervention of public authority in the distribution of the national income, and a certain amount of Keynesian "planning" is a long way from socialism proper, but it is equally far from laissez faire capitalism. Thus there emerges a cleavage between a Right that favors private enterprise and a Left that favors planning and controls.[5]

As one enters the United States Capitol Building from the East Front, the most commonly used entrance, the Senate Chamber is to the right and the House to the left.

In the arrangements of some legislative bodies, at least, the left side is consistently associated with the common people or with opposition to the ruling order, and the right side with established or privileged authority. For over two hundred years the political left has labored unceasingly to convince its contemporaries that it alone truly represents the common people against the exploitative forces of the society in which both struggle for control.

Today, as in 1789, the left declares itself champion of the common people against the propertied class, that is, the owners of industry, the landlords and the corporate world. In the leftist view the most evil obstacles to peace, freedom and love, are profit, private property and greed. The chief Demogorgon is fascism. According to this view, the right, caricatured in leftist cartoons as obese greedy businessmen and feeble brained generals laden with chest medals, cannot be included in the revered class, *the people*, but considered vermin of some subhuman species.

Like the medieval inquisitor who readily meted out the most unspeakable tortures while piously claiming to be but a humble instrument of God, the leftist, given the chance, is willing, if not eager, to perpetrate genocidal murder (Stalin, Hitler, Mao, Kim and Pol Pot) to bring about the unchallenged triumph of his dogma, all in the name of that ever handy sanctimony, *the people*.

The right presents itself as the paladin of law and order; loyal servant of God and country; defender of the faith; preserver of flag, Constitution and American tradition. Partisans of this point of view scorn the left as a force dragging the country into bankruptcy, socialism and bloated government. They maintain the self delusion that they alone defend the last bastion of freedom against the arch-demons, at one time identified as the world communist conspiracy, now just the liberals and progressives.

In general terms, a few exceptions notwithstanding, the left spurns national boundaries, its members considering themselves citizens of the world. Rightists, in contrast, are usually ardent nationalists. Leftists, particularly the communist variety, are often atheists. Rightists commonly defend religion with the possible exceptions of Hitler, Mussolini, and a fair number of Latin American dictators, all political figures usually associated with the right but not conspicuous defenders of religion. Leftists initially proclaim to be nihilists, that is, until they achieve power; the rightists, preservationists. Leftists strive to destroy the prevailing system as a prelude to their glorious triumph; rightists are duty bound to bend their powers toward the preservation of the traditional order.

As they appear on the American political menu, socialism is a slightly diluted totalitarian stew spiced with humanitarian rationalizations and fortified with unsupportable claims for the inevitability of the global adoption of socialist doctrine. Liberalism is a watered-down socialist soup with heavy flavorings of arrogance and phony compassion. Conservatism is served as a thinly filtered liberal broth garnished with toothpick flags and miniature bibles. No matter what one chooses from the menu, authoritarian cyanide remains the principal condiment. The only rational choice is to leave the restaurant.

The archetypes usually used to symbolize the extremes of the political spectrum are communism and fascism represented historically by the former Soviet Union and Nazi Germany. But a spectrum so defined presents unresolvable logical difficulty. Assigning totalitarian regimes to define the extreme ends of a political spectrum implies that all other points within that spectrum represent compromises of the two extremes. All political systems are accordingly seen as variations of statism. The 1789 model, in which delegates seated themselves generally according to their opinions about the French monarchy, at least made some sense. The contemporary model is absurd. Where on this spectrum do we fit today's monarchist, libertarian, pure democrat, anarchist, American Tea Party Patriot, laissez faire capitalist, or the guy who simply yearns to be free of all the political flap and left alone to chase larks of his own choosing?

If we insist on the model that leftists have labored so assiduously to implant and place government by privileged authority on the right and government by the people, i.e. democracy, on the left, then where on this spectrum do we assign Stalin, Mao, Castro, Chavez and their subsequent lineage, or Putin and Xi Jinping? All of these people were, or are certainly considered, honored cardholders of the left, all guilty of oppressing popular movements and denying human rights within their regimes, and all members of privileged oligarchies. Can any of these honestly be described as democratic? Then why are they placed on the left?

To phrase the question more pertinently, why do leftists delude themselves, and attempt to bamboozle everyone else, in presenting the left as the dazzling beacon of democracy? Why in the leftist view have South American "rightwing" dictators been oppressors and murderers, which was certainly true, while the left has been curiously silent about the Castro brothers' dictatorship and the current ones led by Miguel Díaz-Canel in Cuba and Nicolas Maduro, Chavez's successor in Venezuela? All five were or are self proclaimed leftists and every bit as oppressive and lethal to freedom as their presumed rightwing counterparts.

Before the fall of the Soviet Union, communist attempts to seize power around the world were euphemized as struggles for liberation. What can possibly be liberating about a communist dictatorship? Did the horror of Lenin and Stalin "liberate" the suffering Russian people from the lesser horror of Nicholas II? Was the KGB and is its FSB successor more progressive instruments of freedom than the Tsarist Okhrana?

Leftists as a whole preach a complete and fairly consistent doctrine that they insist offers a positive program for the betterment of humanity. They claim motivations of compassion, equality and fair distribution of the Earth's bounty. But the policies of American liberal democrats pose serious fiscal and psychological difficulties that undermine those ideals. First, the rationalizations supporting those policies and their actual implementation contain no limits short of national bankruptcy, which suggests that bankrupting the system as a prelude to all pervasive government may be an actual goal. Secondly, it encourages helplessness, real or feigned, by coddling it, and demonizes the rich with envy disguised as justice.

Rightists, again with the exceptions of Nazism and fascism, espouse defensive postures designed to preserve tradition, that is, flag, bible, Constitution or whatever, with little or no understanding of what these inheritances represent in the present. Rightists vehemently denounce communism but when pressed for a reason why, offer superficial generalities that miss the essence of what communism really is, or condemn it solely on the basis of one of its minor features, its atheism.

Suppose that these unpleasant extremes are set aside momentarily, and the spectrum is redefined only on the basis of American politics. The United States has had no dictatorships, so absolute statism need not anchor the two ends of the American political spectrum. Few would disagree that American liberals could march contentedly under the parade banners of the moderate left. Their programs in progress are undeniably less harsh than those in the former Soviet Union or the current ones in Russia, China, North Korea, Venezuela and Cuba. Toward the other end of this revised spectrum, right-wing ideology at least ostensibly guides the Republican Party but can hardly be identified with fascism.

So, if religious conservatives are employed to define the right node of the American spectrum and liberal democrats hold down the left node, then the band between presumably brackets the whole range of American political opinion.

Or does it?

That religious conservatives are mouthpieces for God, flag, law, order and biblical authority is clearly evidenced from their activities, but do liberal democrats offer an alternative? They spare no effort in presenting themselves as more compassionate, progressive, rational, broadminded, and representative of the people than the rightists they scorn. If liberals can accuse rightists of offering only knee-jerk opposition to whatever liberals consider progress, cannot the rightists justly describe liberals as authoritarian? Is not the ever expanding glut of federal power largely, but by no means exclusively, a progeny of what Americans call liberalism?

The long suffering and grumbling taxpayers, bent under principally liberal inspired levies, have formed grassroots revolts to roll back taxes *in spite of* liberal lamentations that disaster would surely follow. In virtually every case where tax revolt propositions have reached the ballot box or been seriously and broadly discussed, the reigning liberal authorities, in an unmistakably vindictive counterattack, threatened to cut first the services that citizens need most. In these skirmishes no hint is ever heard from liberal quarters that entitlements, countless federal aid programs and welfare doles have reached absurd proportions, or that profligate waste epitomizes liberal administrations, or that cherished liberal programs are counterproductive to the allegedly sought results. Yet these are precisely the excesses that constitute the targets for the tax rebels and the chief sources of frustration to tax paying voters. What value can we assign here to the liberals' claim that they are the true representatives of the people?

Returning to the original model with the two totalitarian poles, are American liberals and conservatives really close to the center of that spectrum and near a balance point of opposing extremes? If the extreme right is totalitarianism maintaining its power by terror and oppression and the extreme left is totalitarianism maintaining its power by terror and oppression, then where can a nonlethal balance point possibly exist between terror and terror? If the communist wants to herd the individual into a monolithic world movement to mold an alleged utopian humanity and the Nazi wishes to force the individual to build the omnipotent perfect State, then of what meaning to the individual is a compromise or center position between these two?

Are American liberalism and conservatism examples of moderation and compromise between the communist and the Nazi? Or do the American liberal and the conservative offer exactly what the communist and the Nazi offer only less of it? Since liberals and conservatives are evidently much better people than communists and nazis, as judged from the administrations that each has controlled, it can be concluded that whatever they offer less of, it must be decidedly unhealthy.

Communist states are far more dangerous to live in than America under liberal administrations has proven to be. The same can be claimed in a comparison of fascists states and American conservative administrations. What then is this political ingredient that serves as a measure of social health and distinguishes the "moderate" center of the spectrum from its lethal end points?

All shades of the left-right spectrum now in popular use possess a single common denominator: State authority. The entire structure is a statist entrapment, for there is no political position anywhere on it or any compromise possible between any two of its elements that does not imply some State control of the individual. Not even that utopian mirage of socialist slogans, pure Athenian democracy where *all* public policy is established by popular vote, can fit within a spectral band saturated with versions of statism. Is the center of the spectrum supposed to float at the null point between two equally deadly and allegedly opposing doctrines? Why not reject statism altogether, abandon the impossible balancing act, and scrap a model that deliberately deceives one into believing that only variations on a theme of statism are among the choices of men?

With otherwise much to offer mankind, conservatism's image has been badly corroded by its marriage to religion and suffers a severe debility from that alliance with the rationally indefensible. Reasonable as they may attempt to present their views, conservative writers, held hostage by religious doctrinaires within their ranks, cannot shake off that association with the irrational. Their most pointed arguments bounce off their intended targets like toy arrows tipped with foam balls. Their force is weakened by an authoritarian irrationalism not that much different from the one that infects the left. The two just want us to kneel to different authorities.

In permitting the left to polarize the issues that divide the world into left versus right, liberal versus conservative, we create a dangerously misleading mirage. The central problems of our day, although appearing diverse and insoluble, do congeal into two opposing fundamentals, but not the two that the polit-ical concepts of left and right convey. The left unquestionably represents one of the nodes, collectivism, to which the only possible antipode is individualism. But what has become accepted as representative of the right, the presumed opposition to the left, smacks not of individualism, but a mishmash of contra-dictions, religious dogma, unconvincing defenses of tradition and guilt-ridden mimics of the left's baseless assertions.

The commonly cited spectrum, with fascism at one end and communism at the other, not only fails miserably to accommodate monarchy, anarchy, laissez faire capitalism, communal living, hermiting on an island, or other historical and speculative systems, but is deliberately contrived to lull the unwary into accepting the farce that only compromises between fascism and communism are possible. These two are not opposing poles in any mean-ingful spectrum of thought, but Siamese twin ogres joined at the head and sharing the small brain of a tyrant.

> The major flaw in all of this is that fascism, properly understood, is not a phenomenon of the right at all. Instead, it is, and always has been, a phenomenon of the left. This fact — an inconvenient truth if ever there was one — is obscured in our time by the equally mistaken belief that fascism and communism are opposites. In reality, they are closely related, historical competitors for the same constituents, seeking to dominate and control the same social space.[6]

Since the whole of political history chronicles the struggle between the individual and the State, i.e., between freedom and organized force, a rational political spectrum would depict increments of statism from zero to totalitarianism, the absolute individual to the absolute State. In this model the Siamese twins, communism and fascism, anchor the extreme left node where they belong, and the island hermit who marches only to his own drum anchors the right end. These make an impractical trio to be sure but at least make sense in that they define a spectrum that permits gradations of state authority over the individual.

If we adhere to this model, slightly to the left of the hermit would appear a simple community of individuals who have forsworn any political structure at all and successfully live by the single rule that they will not interfere in one another's affairs.

A point a bit further to the left can be represented by a small community of people who have agreed among themselves to rotate in a role, or appoint an authority, empowered to enforce contracts, try and detain criminals and organize any necessary defense. Thus emerges an incipient State.

Somewhere further along this revised spectrum, moving from right to left, lies a point where the State is no longer totally authorized by the people whose varied contributions give it strength and meaning. Moving leftward beyond this point, the individual suffers increasing State regulation of his affairs until finally the left extremity is attained, total State control of every detail of existence, even reaching to the inviolate privacy of the mind.

Stalin's Russia, Hitler's Germany, Mao's China, Pol Pot's Kampuchea (Cambodia), Kim's North Korea, Castro's Cuba, and the novels *1984* by George Orwell and *Brave New World* by Aldous Huxley paint accurate but ominous pictures of the left node of a meaningful spectrum.

An example that could fit comfortably near the right end of such a spectrum and still be viable in a modern complex industrial society has never existed. It can however be described as a nation of responsible independent adults who have gained from the bitter lessons of history so healthy a suspicion of government that the one they have created is a severely limited, definitively circumscribed, shackled, bound, gagged, blindfolded and castrated automaton that functions solely to protect the citizens from human predators. This is, to be sure, a most illiberal picture in the American proactive government sense of the concept *liberal*.

By pushing the Nazi brand of socialism into an artificially right node role as archetype of absolute evil, and then ignoring, minimizing or divorcing themselves from the even worse barbarities of the communist brand of socialism, socialists have managed to delude themselves and a sizable fraction of their listeners into accepting the lie that their system does not rest ultimately on unrestrained force. Like a killer who hollers "murder!" as he hides a bloody dagger up his sleeve, socialists can point aghast to the millions murdered by the Nazi gorgon and by that diversion draw attention away from themselves as the gorgon's even more bloody brothers.

A point on a meaningful left-right political spectrum could be located by the degree of authority applied to it. As a tongue-in-cheek suggestion, it could be measured by the percentage of the GDP poured into governments at all levels, or the percentage of law enforcement officials in the total population.[7]

The absurdity of the current left-right spectrum emerges plainly revealed out of the political chaos of Latin America, played out late in the last century in Argentina, Chile, Nicaragua and Salvador, and now vigorous once again in Venezuela and budding in Chile. In the last century "right-wing" generals forced their way into power on the pretext of saving their countries from communism. In this century the ardent leftists, the Castro brothers, the late Hugo Chavez and their successors, indistinguishable from their "right-wing" progenitors, found a new demon, the United States. They promised to usher in a new order of peace, prosperity, freedom and equality, which of course did not happen and cannot happen in Cuba or Venezuela under Díaz-Canel or Madura respectively or anyone of like mind.

When the inevitable failures of authoritative "solutions" bring yet more ruin, the generals (or sergeants or whoever) will again rise to "save" the people and the pendulum will swing "right." The wearisome cycles of South American politics, or those of anywhere else, are doomed to continue until either the government in question grows so powerful and oppressive that opposition is impossible (China and North Korea), or the people who empower that government stop looking for political remedies to problems that largely result from their own refusal to assume individual responsibility for the courses of their lives.

The Republican and Democratic parties have foisted on the American people the alternatives of religion or the welfare state, omnipotent God or all intrusive government, or some mix of the two, grim choices for those precious few of us who do not want either one. One side of our ludicrous contemporary debate asserts what the State ought to force everyone to do, the other side what God wants us to do. Trapped between two terrible lies, Americans face the deadly alternatives of ancient statist collectivism posing in a modern garb of humanitarian liberalism, and equally ancient theocracy hiding its unbroken record of intolerance beneath an anguished concern for the erosion of traditional values.

As with an individual neurosis, a person's refusal to see that his methods of dealing with reality do not work serves only to perpetuate the failed results of continuously acting on the same beliefs. Albert Einstein commented that the definition of insanity is doing something over and over again and expecting a different result. Does this not describe our endless failed attempts to erect the perfect welfare state?

Those Americans who promote the parental state, my preferred term for the welfare state, have by default held the high moral ground for the better part of a century, and forced into retreat those antagonists who offer little but religion to defend their arguments. Religion itself has been in headlong retreat for centuries, at least in the West, pummeled by assaults from quite another opponent, science, and now lacks the authority to defend anything.

The left advances unopposed because the wimpy non-force popularly identified as its enemy fails to grasp the essential issue of the battle and either jousts with the windmills of its dogma or wanders about in a bewildered half-hearted search for the battlefield. The real enemies of the left comprise a small minority: the individualist, the iconoclast and the entrepreneur, and remain disorganized, discouraged and only recently enlightened to the nature and magnitude of the evil they face. Not least among the paradoxes with which they grapple, is the perceived need to organize individualism into an effective war machine without transforming it into another version of the very collectivist antipode against which reason struggles in mortal combat.

The raging battle for men's minds is being fought today principally between two groups peddling rival mythologies. Finding truth amidst the melee will daunt even the most determined thinkers. Models for the conflict can be found in the French and Russian Revolutions. Neither side in either contest valued truth beyond expediency and morality sunk into mutual murder. The only action a sane person could have taken in either of these conflicts would have been to get out if possible and if not, try hard to achieve invisibility.

Our present debate rages not between liberal and conservative but between secular authority and religious authority, the socialist myth or the theistic myth, an oligarchy of morally posturing leftists pretending to represent the people or an oligarchy of morally self righteous clerics pretending to represent the revealed truth. We float rudderless between the Scylla of a potential Stalinist nightmare and the Charybdis of bigoted theocracy. We must choose and we much choose neither of these.

Liberals and conservatives talk past one another. Liberals see no danger in the ever expanding government that so disturbs conservatives. Conservatives can't see that arguments derived from religion or what some founding father had to say no longer have any power over the ideas that excite liberals or that move the world.

We must stop centering our political debate around the conflict between the conservative and the liberal. It would be much better to consider if individuals should have to bear alone the consequences of their own shortcomings and failures, however acquired, or be compensated for their disadvantages and losses by the rest of the community via the taxing power of a parental government.

The debate then focuses on establishing a balance between personal desires on behalf of, and obligations to, self and loved ones on one side, and duties owed to the general community on the other. The exact location of that balance point never has been reached and possibly can never reach an acceptable compromise, much less a consensus. Nevertheless we face the need to locate that point. The evasion of the effort succinctly sums up the individual versus the collective or man versus the State conflicts that have raged unabated for millennia.

Philosophers expounding their ideas without an adequate understanding of their subject, real people, produce off-the-mark or ludicrous tomes. Psychology and other sciences that study the mind and the brain, though woefully inadequate, still provide our most promising sources for the crucial understandings on which any meaningful and applicable philosophy must rest.

Grapplers for power from the authoritarian extremes of right and left resemble brother princes vying for a soon to be vacated throne. Neither represent anything but naked malevolence. Both are equally ugly and both equally deadly.

The choices of people who truly desire freedom cannot be exercised by voting in a contest among rival statists. Only the rejection of statism, and that also implies rejection of a political spectrum that offers only compromises with that nightmare, will preserve our legacy of freedom.

NOTES

1   John Hall Stewart, *A Documentary Survey of the French Revolution*, The Macmillan Co., 1951, p39.
2   Stewart, p86.
3   Stewart, p270.
4   Maurice Duverger, *The French Political System*, The University of Chicago Press, 1958, p133.
5   Duverger, p133.
6   Jonah Goldberg, *Liberal Fascism*, Broadway Books, New York, 2009, page 7
7   Wikipedia in June 2018 listed dozens of federal law enforcement agencies including those in the military employing a total of over 100,000 officers. The figure excludes state and local law enforcement organizations.

OUR POLITICAL CONTROVERSIES

Excerpted and revised from *America's Suicide,* **2nd Edition**

MOST PEOPLE CLAIM GOD EXISTS. Others say the concept is a comforting but archaic and destructive illusion long past any utility it may have once brought mankind.

One affirms the value of private property; another counters that private property serves only the rich at the expense of the common people. "Property is theft," claims an old leftist cliché.

One side of another argument upholds the value of unregulated entrepreneurial ambition and its attendant pursuit of profit; still others scorn the idea as exploitative, rapacious, callously insensitive to the real needs of people or to the health of our planet which belongs to all of us and our posterity.

Still another proclaims human individuality and its right to pursue noble or infamous ends free of any notions of social contract. Nonsense scoffs the opposition. Man is a social animal bound to his species in an implicit but unseen natural interconnecting web of mutual love and support. We are all in this together, continues this viewpoint, and the most able among us must be compelled if necessary to reach out to the least able instead of selfishly devoting innate, and therefore accidental, superior talents to accumulating meaningless acquisitions.

Distrust of government was an axiom that accounts for the intricate counterbalances woven into the United States Constitution. People who retain that distrust want to confine government functions within strict Constitutional limits. Other thinkers view the Constitution as a "living document" and government as a uniquely qualified force to enact a more just distribution of the wealth of the community.

Political freedom conveys no meaning to those lacking economic equality, insists one group. Economic inequality exists as a fact of Nature, ripostes the opposing group, and efforts to arbitrarily redistribute economic realities according to some egalitarian scheme destroys everyone's freedom.

Reason, employing its handmaiden, science, is our only guide to truth, asserts one view. What blather sneers the opposing view. Many roads to knowledge open before the wondering spirit. Reason easily leads to any preconceived conclusion and cannot begin to penetrate the most troubling questions of life. It should confine its inquiries to the utilitarian, leaving our timeless *whys* to ancient and modern sages contemplating the universal mysteries of the cosmic all.

Conservatives see liberals as eager to seize every crisis - real, exaggerated or invented - to expand the government and their own influence and rationalize larceny to fund their spending schemes.

Liberals see conservatives as reactionary, chained to obsolete beliefs and traditions, and knee-jerk opposed to everything that liberals consider progressive.

Is there any truth to any of these charges? Will anyone on either side of these controversies at least concede the possibility that the other side has a point worthy of serious consideration? Is there no way to resolve this interminable and tedious acrimony?

Are we so wedded to our respective views of reality as to preclude a satisfactory meeting of minds? Must we forever glare at one another in the forums of social dispute? Hurl invectives, threats, irrelevancies, non sequiturs and arguments untethered from evidence or historical context? Maneuver our side of the argument to enhance influence over reason? Gather partisans to

weigh in on the side of force? Sneak our beliefs and prejudices into the legislature with the intent to preempt the opposition and apply the power of law
to upset the balance of discussion? Is there no way to resolve these conflicts
by drawing upon objective data and historical lessons? Are we stuck with the
sole expedient of considering the relative forces of the contending gangs?

Everybody holds a patent on reality. The communist, socialist, liberal,
conservative, cleric, atheist, libertarian, laissez faire capitalist, anarchist,
pragmatist, you name it, all claim exclusive possession of the correct inter-
pretation of reality. With all those right answers out there, every one of them
in conflict with every other one, somebody is sure lying like hell.

The comfortable assurances sought in doctrinal beliefs come with a steep
price. The believer fails to take more realistic actions to mitigate the pains and
disappointments of life and deludes him or herself with the conviction that
the professed doctrine promises the solution to worldly troubles instead of
being a major contributor to the very deleterious conditions that the believer
yearns to escape. Unquestioned doctrines are their own worst enemy.

Imagine a group of fundamentalist Christians, devout Muslims, ortho-
dox Jews, communists, nazis, anarchists, monarchists, mystics, skeptics,
atheists, laissez faire capitalists, and a ranting psychotic posturing as the
heir to the throne of Charlemagne all sitting at, walking around, or banging
their fists on a conference table in a huge hotel room. A young psychologist
wanders by mistake into the room while looking for the rest room. Momentarily forgetting the purpose that brought her there, she stands transfixed by
the mayhem, fascinated by the sudden fortuitous opportunity to study her
favorite subject and fulfill an old desire to submit a scholarly paper to the
Journal of Madness.

These people, except the one there by mistake, came there not to listen,
reflect, examine their own convictions and motives and offer considered
judgments, but to proselytize, denounce, overwhelm, cajole, insult, and
stentoriously proclaim the superiority of their respective orthodoxies. Each
prophesies imminent global catastrophe for failure to adopt the proposed
doctrine. Each declares himself the devoted disciple of revealed truth, an

undaunted warrior on the side of reality or scientifically determined destiny, and ordained by God, ineluctable history or the positions of the stars to carry the true gospel to the ignorant masses.

Not one of these people sees his beliefs as a set of interlocking viewpoints subject to exposure, insult and injury in an open discussion. The beliefs simply are. To refute them is to refute God, Nature, reality, historical determinism, or whatever unquestionable authority the believer invokes to bind his assertions to unassailable logic. To their advocates, orthodoxies are fused with self evident definitions and therefore assumed synonymous with reality. Like the law of gravity, they are experienced as absolute, axiomatic, irrefutable, automatized, unthinkable, and therefore not thought about and therefore unconscious.

Here lurks the root of war.

Does truth find any respect here? Who is right? Who wrong? Why? Who among the disputants honors both supporting and refuting factual data over groundless opinion? Who arrives to listen, learn and offer considered judgment and who to preach, threaten and overwhelm? How can committed disputants reconcile? How does right prevail over error, good over evil, reasoned discourse over naked force, objective inquiry over entrenched and belligerent orthodoxy, and tolerance over bigotry? What commits a mind so tenaciously to a conclusion that its defense must be contrived from evidence first filtered through the fabric of the very view being defended, while contrary evidence is scorned, dismissed, contorted or ignored? Must the final arbiter of resolute adversaries always be a shouting or a shooting war? Will the mind ever reach the point when it can consider all evidence in the light of reason and reach a provisional conclusion while remaining alert to the possibility of being wrong? Must the mind evolve significantly further before it can grasp principles necessary to avoid its own folly?

Can two very different minds ever reconcile? Is it possible even if they both try very hard and commit themselves to honest and respectful mutual exploration?

When one disputant asks another, "How can we settle this? Why can't we agree and get along?" What he really means is, "Why are you so obstinate that you can't see it my way?" Or (secretly) "What's wrong with this jerk; what world does he live in?"

Irreconcilable disagreements usually have at least a few disruptive elements that prevent accord such as:

1. Truth is not respected or considered culturally dependent.

2. Facts presented by either side are considered by the other side as irrelevant to the discussion, wrong or social constructs.

3. Not all relevant facts can be brought to the discussion either because they are not known by one or both disputants and in any case cannot all fit inside one head.

4. People heavily load their arguments with their respective beliefs that trump any facts that conflict with those beliefs.

5. Both opposing arguments might well contain bits of truth and falsehood but with no reliable means of determining the weight of either.

6. Statistical data are cherry picked and subject to conflicting interpretations again biased by one's unquestioned beliefs.

7. Disputants often dishonestly adhere to a clandestine agenda disguised behind reassuring smiles and nods.

Imagine a committed atheistic communist talking to a fundamentalist religious conservative discussing limited government and free markets. Each of course sees the other as at least deluded, maybe dishonest and at the very worst, wrong-headed.

These two each came into the world with genetic and cultural predispositions that at least permitted them to grow up and argue with one another. But from the day of birth to the day of meeting, each life has taken its own path. Each step on that path, each experience of adventure, joy, risk, love, hate, rejection, disappointment, pain, disease, injury, achievement or failure cast a step the past aggregate of which urged toward the next step. A time arrives when the two paths have diverged to such a degree that the two travelers through life can scarcely understand one another even if reared in the same language and culture. Even assuming extraordinary intelligence and good will on both sides, each would have to delve deep into the past experiences and root assumptions of the other, most of the latter long since automatized and therefore unconscious, to gain a modicum of appreciation for the other viewpoint. Is such a journey possible? Increase the number of disputants beyond two and misunderstandings multiply exponentially.

Does anyone really want to change his or her basic assumptions unless compelled to do so by a dilemma that demands a decision between two terrible choices? An example might take the form of an unpleasant compromise with a repugnant but powerful and threatening doctrine. Chamberlain's compromise with Hitler, leaving Czechoslovakia to its fate, fits the description.

Another one developed not long after WWII. Centuries of ever more brutal internecine wars among Europeans forced a few of the more circum-spect citizens to face the reality that they could not go on like this. They *had* to find some nonviolent means to resolve their differences or face continental suicide. The European Economic Community and the later European Union resulted. They still shout at one another but have for the most part stopped shooting each other. The Balkan Wars in the 1990s have been the exception.

We have mainly focused our political debates on left versus right, demo-crat versus republican, socialist versus capitalist, or collectivist versus indi-vidualist. But we argue in the wrong arena. We should instead be asking, "how does this thing up here work?" Tap the side of your head while asking this question. Why do we find it so excruciatingly difficult to question our beliefs? To understand and sympathize with someone else's sharply differing point of view? To weigh the pro and con evidence concerning some issue and choose rationally? Must we always allow passion to rule reason even to the destruction of our species?

The ontological and epistemological questions posed by the Greeks two and a half millennia ago, still valid and still unanswered, rapidly approach the time when they *must* be answered. We have arrived at a point when we are quite capable of obliterating ourselves and a distressing number of nuts out there have clearly demonstrated a willingness to do just that. How many more Stalins, Hitlers, Maos and Pol Pots, now armed with nuclear and pathogenic bombs, can the world withstand? Russia's invasion of Ukraine, the nuclear armed lunatics that presently run North Korea and the rising tide of violent Islam add further weight to the argument.

The questions of which political party or whose religion or view of mankind must prevail must be preceded by the much more fundamental questions raised by the ancient Greeks and never adequately answered: What is the nature of man? What is good? What is truth? What is the proper function of government? What do we know? How do we know what we know? These and derivative questions must continue, as they have been doing, to pass from the realm of philosophy into that of psychology and brain physiology, the disciplines that study the mind.

Any ideology that tries by whatever means to silence its critics identifies itself as a religion, exposes its intellectual vacuity and deserves dismissal from further respect.

Our search outward for the ideal political system has been a grave misdirection. The perfect governing system, even if such is possible, cannot emerge until we understand that which is to be governed. We must first peer within. How do we write a political philosophy for man until we know what man is? The answer to that question must come from psychology and related inquires. Among the great number of human problems, very few, if any, are resolvable by government which usually makes them worse. Any activity that the government undertakes will inevitably prove bureaucratic, inefficient, expensive, averse to innovation, and notorious for perfunctory job performance especially where it comes face to face with the public it is supposed to serve.

We cannot answer all the fundamental questions about ourselves anytime soon. Our emotion loaded preferences much too easily preempt honest thought. We then draft that subordinated thought into the service of justifying the preference. Only the most brutally honest escape that circular trap and even then, imperfectly. We do not so much think as rationalize and recycle.

The answers to our political dilemmas and conflicts paradoxically are not political, but individually psychological. No political party on Earth has the slightest chance of providing them.

Our political disagreements are so intractable because we persist in seeing the nature of human conflict in the wrong terms. Both sides of the contemporary political debate see only their own rectitude and only the errors of the opposition. Both are simultaneously right and wrong.

Counterintuitively, political animosity cannot be eliminated by political discussion nor social problems resolved by sociologists and news commentators. Our fundamental differences are not by nature epistemological and therefore not resolvable by education and debate, however polite, but psychological, and therefore resolvable only by individual self examination. Problems of the world are rooted in the nature of man himself, most specifically his capacity to so easily fool himself. Resolution lies not in a political direction, but toward greater individual self-understanding and acceptance of personal responsibility. Our nation, in step with the rest of the world, has been marching in the opposite direction for much of our history, particularly in the decades since the beginning of the twentieth century

If psychology was ever the handmaiden of philosophy, their relative positions are now reversed. Further progress in philosophy awaits a more effective means to penetrate the unconscious and open a window into the guarded recesses of each human soul. People are very devoted to the beliefs that guide their political choices. We should be less impassioned about which candidate or political party carries the next election and much more curious about the genetic, psychological and experiential influences that led us to that preference. And is that preference right? Why? What one *feels* is right sheds little light on this crucial deliberation. Before they vote people should ask themselves a difficult question: "Are the social problems that I decry successfully addressed by my view of reality or in part caused by the principles that I hold to be true?"

We form many of our most enduring impressions at an age when knowledge, judgment and reason wait undeveloped in defenseless immaturity. The impressions then solidify into a received and accepted view of reality. They are almost never seen as optional adoptions.

To cite only one example of how a very early childhood environment can powerfully sway the much later choice of a political viewpoint, consider a toddler who hears from his mother - the deified giver of all life and truth - daily assurances of his worthlessness and inadequacy. The horrific task for him to later overcome such a legacy is not difficult to imagine. But as terrible as such circumstances may inflame our sense of injustice, the child and much later grownup adult *appear* to be grappling with mere words, albeit authoritative words, but still words that represent identifiable concepts that reason is presumably free to reject.

But a mother's capacity for cruelty does not suddenly well up upon arrival of her child's capacity to understand her words. She had to have been expressing that attitude from his birth and forcing that cruelty into his defenseless forming mind as countless non verbal impressions absorbed by him as vague and diffuse feelings, likely of rejection, insecurity or irritability, and later, during the language developing months, approximated by him in immature verbal concepts. Humiliating words easily drop into place in a budding defenseless mind long since conditioned to receive them.

A small child who cannot yet understand language is nevertheless profoundly influenced by tone of voice, the absence or presence of anxiety or fear in the environment, affection or rejection, playfulness or dejection, tranquility or violence and a hundred other factors. That seedbed of influences begins forming the foundation of a person's much later ingrained and unexamined assumptions.

By the time a toddler is able to understand the message, "you are bad," the words are received as no more than a corroboration of what has been inculcated and "known" almost from birth and therefore tragically accepted with neither reflection nor question. The preverbal environment has preconditioned the defenseless mind to readily accept much later spoken messages. When the child repeats, "I am bad," he is verbally approximating and symbolizing a feeling much earlier embedded in the mind, fused with self-identity and therefore far more difficult to later challenge with by now seriously handicapped reasoning.

The preverbal emotional and mental impressions that will form the foundation of the toddler's future personality are already much more complex and fused into his self-identity than his limited language skills can possibly articulate and might, along with many people, remain so for life. For him the statement, "I am bad," is not a deliberated assessment of self, but an identification of self with non-goodness. This might at first appear as a mere quibble about some exaggerated difference, but the point here is to establish the distinction between an idea, theory, assessment or judgment perceived as such and therefore subject to examination and refutation; and an idea, theory, belief, assessment or judgment *not* seen as such but automatically, unconsciously, unquestioningly accepted as reality. The first remains open to reflection. The second just *is* and integrated into one's assessment of self.

To the much later adult struggling to understand painful and inexplicable emotions, any number of reassurances of his personal value will spend themselves like surf pounding a rock cliff. What appears as obstinacy in a listener for failure to heed helpful advice is in reality the brain's resistance to sudden rearrangement. A surf will eventually wear away a cliff, but we should not look for speed in the process, only resistance.

Evil grows its roots in the rich soil of ignorance. Human beings lack the knowledge, especially self-awareness, to grasp reality with doubt-free assurance. They compensate by clinging to reassuring but more often than not false beliefs about their inner and outer worlds.

Nature does not finger-paint her secrets on the bottoms of clouds for all to see. Any realistic degree of certainty can only be purchased with arduous research, patient observation and honest deduction, daunting requirements for even the most capable minds and way beyond the reach of the least capable. Much more easily can certainty be counterfeited from the fabric of orthodoxy, then belligerently defended with subordinate reason shanghaied into service as rationalizer.

Are we rational creatures? Yes, but reasoning is not a dominant mental process for a great many people. We struggle through life as semi-conscious easily frightened creatures bereft of reliable self-knowledge and who live in a pervasively dangerous and bewildering world that nevertheless exacts terrible penalties, including great anguish and death, for making wrong choices. That imposes an unreachably high price on correct decisions. In consequence certainty assumes vital importance, while the human being's inability to see himself at all clearly leaves him with a distressing capacity to lie to himself. He prefers to invent comforting but unsupportable certainties, especially religious and political ones.

Human evolution has only partially advanced and hopefully we will not do something stupid enough to interrupt the process. The cognitive and rational part of our human nature so often seems the weaker part waging a continuous losing war against powerful emotional tyrants. Much of what we do is impulsive and compulsive with a lip service bow to reason now and then to sanction and sanitize our decisions, give them at least a veneer of considered thought and permit us to call ourselves rational animals.

I do not condemn reason. It is the only weapon we have to fight in the compulsion versus volition war that rages ceaselessly in varying intensities inside all of us. I only lament the inadequacies of reason and the ease with which we subvert it. A good many people surrender to their compulsions, endlessly recycle the same ideas, stretch the same few behavior patterns over all life's challenges, and call the process reasoning. Still others consciously renounce reason, rely totally on feelings and deny that they derive from one another.

Innumerable observers of human nature have never ceased to remind us that passion rules reason. These people argue that reason easily stretches over the ridiculous, leaving not a tiny wrinkle of doubt. We have often observed reason with equal facility drafted into the service of anything from the absurd to the profound. People argue with equal passion and unassailable logic for anything from astrology to Zoroastrianism without so much as a whisper of acknowledgment that they cannot reconcile their beliefs with observed data. The data are simply filtered and distorted to conform to the belief system.

Mankind's most dire need coincides with one of our least recognized ones. We need nothing so desperately as a clear view of ourselves. I mean this not in a collective sociological or political sense, but in the often evaded struggle for individual self-awareness, the kind of awareness that asks what genetic, nurturing, familial, societal and political forces and personal choices have pushed me in the direction I have taken and toward what will these influences urge me in the future?

People routinely evade the pain associated with the inward journey by focusing outward toward the readily identifiable faults of their respective societies instead of inward to expose the denied faults of self. But the introspective direction holds more promise in searching for ways to mitigate the discords that torment our world.

We cannot identify the hidden contact points of social friction unless we better understand ourselves as individuals living in, contributing to, and drawing from the social interactions that create that friction. One's political, economic and social interactions evolve from assumptions about oneself and one's role in the world and therefore find root in one's own psychology. Sociological speculations must be firmly anchored to observable individual psychology if such speculations are not to sink into a morass of sociobabble.

A shift in the focus of attention away from the sociopolitical and toward the individual elicits considerable discomfort in people who look to social reforms to ameliorate suffering and think it much easier to imagine, and join political action groups devoted to, changing the world rather than probe inward for the sources of personal discontent and social awkwardness. To such people the world will always appear in great need of their respective prescriptions for a better society.

The principal anguish of humankind is not rooted in poverty, avarice, disease, war, inequality, overpopulation, environmental disaster, pollution or any of the other red herrings darting across the contemporary stage, but in a profound ignorance of what we are coupled to the limitless human capacity to self deceive. The often willful blindness of the inward gazing eye is *the* fundamental human debility from which all other human caused suffering derives. If we persist in trying to understand a problem within the context and terms of an erroneous theory, understanding will forever elude us.

The majority of human beings peer not under the surface of who they are and how they got that way. They manage to convince themselves that they have overcome their unconscious impulses and compulsions or at least reduced them to irrelevance, or pursue the mirage of some belief system, usually religious and/or political. These people twitch about at the bottom ends of puppet strings manipulated above life's stage by the invisible and therefore unacknowledged hands of root family, culture and unexamined belief. It is always easier to join some religious or political group dedicated to changing the world than to search inward at one's self for the sources of dissatisfaction. The drivel that we are captains of our souls and determine our own fates[1] shrinks to a ridiculous self delusion in the minds of those who abhor self examination. Self determination belongs to the self examined, a non-spectator event with a minuscule fan club.

Our goal should be to mitigate the human curse, not search for some forever receding social or political ideal that will presumptuously guarantee justice and tranquility. We must search for and find better ways to reveal the individual to himself or herself sufficiently to enable that self to choose freedom while fully understanding both the choice and its price.

We arrive at a dilemma. If a committed defense of one's cherished beliefs stands in the way of resolving differences with other people, each of whom is also bound to some personal set of beliefs, and people are demonstrably resistant to questioning their beliefs, how are social conflicts to be resolved without hatred and violence?

Do we simply live and let live, an often heard cliché? But then what principles would guide courts toward just decisions and legislatures toward fair laws? What generally accepted principles add their strength to a society's structure and give it meaning and legitimacy? Some principles have to govern even with the eclipse of some other equally compelling ones. How do we choose which shall prevail? How can we set aside our prejudices just enough to allow the lessons of history to teach us which principles work better?

Some societies in the past have worked demonstrably better than others, a considerable number confined to the same territorial borders and vitalized by the interactions of many of the same people. Germany immediately before and immediately after 1933 furnishes an excellent illustration. What made the sudden difference? A set of beliefs, some quietly dormant for generations, others slowly gaining strength, suddenly flared into ascendancy in the midst of economic upheaval and general distrust of the preceding set of beliefs.

Another example is Russia before and after 1917.

The dominant belief system that characterizes a society at any given moment resembles a resultant vector of all the personal beliefs of the individuals who make up that society. Also evident is that the prevailing beliefs in a society greatly determine how a child is raised and therefore what beliefs the later adult will accept and then contribute to the perpetuation of those same beliefs. So does the society determine what one holds true, or does each individual in the society contribute to the generally accepted doctrines? Evidently both are true. But society is an abstraction and people are real. Therefore to change a strongly held belief, whether individual or societal, implies getting inside people's heads. More specifically, individuals must get inside their own heads, a task greeted with about the same enthusiasm as an appointment with a brain surgeon.

Despite the powerful influences that push us thither and yon, once reaching the age that law defines as adulthood, each of us is entirely responsible for our every thought and action and from that principle there is no escape. No infirmity, no disease, no addiction, no physical or mental incapacity, rotten childhood, dysfunctional family, impoverishment, cries of helplessness, bad luck, unconscious compulsions, nothing, absolutely nothing, lets you off the hook. You may appeal for help and many might respond depending on the merits of you and your predicament. But no one *owes* free anything to anyone beyond childhood or voluntary consent. At first this might strike one as an injustice, or at least a contradiction of what has been written above. How can we be pushed by unseen internal and outside forces yet still be held responsible for what we do?

See the essay on Justice.

Built-in and environmental forces that nudge us here and there are influences, albeit strong ones, but not determinants. Reason plays in a game with the dice loaded against it, but it is not powerless, especially if we stay alert that reason plays against loaded dice. Our limited capacity to clearly see ourselves and our circumstances relieves us of nothing.

Seeing the nature of a problem, however grim, must be the first step toward resolution. Without that first step we wander about in a fog grasping at whatever answers promise to assuage the anxiety of not knowing. Those answers do not have to make sense. They just have to allay fear and have often been placed in the realm of the supernatural, that is, beyond the reach of reason, then defended with rituals and deadly threats.

We do reason. We just don't do it very well and much too easily trump it with emotionally charged preconceptions, especially unquestioned beliefs. So how are we to overcome such a severe handicap?

Faced with our inadequate capacities and drawing on our own fertile imagination, we have always expanded our capacities with invention. Not possessed of a coat of fur, we fashion and wear warm clothing and adapt ourselves to every climate. Not able to run as fast as a horse, we tame and ride the horse and later invent ships and automobiles. Unable to match the bird's soaring freedom, we invent flying machines. Lacking the sharp vision of the eagle, we invent binoculars and telescopes.

Centuries ago a few brave Greek thinkers, suspicious if not contemptuous of the supernatural and whimsical answers to the myriad riddles that Nature threw all about them, began to respect evidence and formulate theories that conformed to what they were seeing and did not require the intrigues of capricious gods. Later thinkers, uncomfortably aware of how easily emotion trumps reason, developed the empirical method of observation, hypothesis, experimentation and verification. The more honest of these thinkers remained, and still remain, allegiant to that method even in face of bitter disappointment when experiments fail to corroborate a favored theory. It has become the proven methodology of hard science that rescued us from mystical tyranny and ushered in a technological world that would have astounded our forebears of only a century or so ago. But the method cannot be more perfect than the humans who apply it. We remain vulnerable to our passions.

Alternatives to this discomforting picture do appear on the horizon of an optimist but can easily succumb to our predilection for answers that momentarily feel good but brought low by subsequent reality.

The first of these is to encourage greater vigilance of the power that our genetic endowment and past and present environmental immersion has over our individual thinking ability.

Second, develop a greater respect for the scientific method and apply it even where it has traditionally been absent or dismissed as irrelevant, that is, in the speculations of philosophers, politicians, sociologists, journalists, religious leaders and other expositors of human behavior.

Third, we have taken the first few baby steps toward developing thinking machines, a possibility that has passed beyond science fiction. Scientists, engineers and writers devoted to this endeavor refer to it as artificial intelligence and it is as exciting to some as frightening to others. Whether it emerges as marvel or menace will depend on the very reasoning capacity that so many of us would dearly love to enhance.

Unlike demagogues, of whom the world suffers a surplus, I have no deeply reassuring political solutions to offer. I have, however, identified the road along which our most needed solutions will be found: the road of self discovery, the road of individual responsibility, the road least travelled.

If the twenty-first century is to escape the genocidal horrors of its predecessor, it must become a century of the mind, a century of self discovery, of penetrations into the labyrinths of thought, of invention of the means to break out of the personal prisons constructed from the experiences of our nurturing years, of rejection of those philosophies that chain our minds to theistic and political myths and thus impoverish our overly brief lives. It is becoming rapidly incumbent upon us to discover the magic bullet that will open our minds to ourselves. We must conquer our severest, and what is becoming our deadliest, handicap. We must discover what we are.

NOTES

1   Presumably originating in the poem *Invictus* by the 19th Century British poet William Ernest Henley.

THE CYCLE OF DEMOCRACY

S OMEONE ONCE WROTE, later quoted by Churchill, that "democracy is the worst form of government except for all the others." What a grim indictment of our political structures. That democracy is the least bad of all the tried alternatives should not blind us to its considerable shortcomings.

I see this country in sharp decline. Like many people who see the same and offer their explanations, I have for some years thought and written about the causes of this dystopian trend and offer my view on the what and the why. I see the current trend as part of an endlessly repeating cycle with variations that come with each cycle.

What defines the elements in the cycle? Where are we in the cycle? How did we get to this invidious moral state? Focusing only on the last four centuries:

A. From the Industrial Revolution, science, and entrepreneurial capitalism came great wealth.

B. From great wealth came great disparity of wealth concentrated in the more able, intelligent and ambitious.

C. From great disparity of wealth came:

1. privileged kids growing up with deficient acceptance of the responsibility to work productively to earn a living, but rather arrogant presumptions of moral superiority and right to rule.

2. kids growing up with unconscious guilt for unearned afflu-
   ence assuaged not by giving their money away, but yours. They
   glow with magnanimity with other people's money and enjoy
   applause and votes from the beneficiaries. The posturing delivers a hell of a payoff.

3. envy and cries of unfairness and exploitation from those who
   feel oppressed, left out and see no deficiency in themselves.

D. From envy came convictions of entitlement.

E. From those convictions arose demagoguery.

F. Then came the many variants of socialism posing as liberal, progressive, just and compassionate to disguise craving for authoritative
   office, pretense of moral superiority and larceny.

G. Over our immediate future looms the specter of socialism which
   will bring the uniformity of universal impoverishment, dependency,
   irresponsibility, entitlement, apathy and finally dictatorship.

I fear that humanity must pass through endless cycles of oppression,
despotism, insurrection and war; then reconstruction, freedom, democracy,
explosion of creativity, industriousness, prosperity and great disparity of
wealth that parallels the great disparities of ability and ambition; then envy,
cries of unfairness and presumed social injustice.

Then come the pandering demagogues preaching hypocritical compassion, criminalizing wealth, rationalizing larceny, seductively assuring entitlement, and disdaining traditional values. This inevitably results in endless
contention, corruption of words vital to understanding freedom, honor and
justice; moral anarchy, ruinous taxation and inflation, universal bankruptcy,
political disintegration and chaos, and panicked clamoring for a savior from
self inflicted folly.

Then the savior rises up like a specter of doom wearing the smiles of a
tyrant and kick starts the cycle over again.

I did not invent any of this. Parts of the cycle can be seen played out in the history of this land from colonial times to the present day, in Germany from Bismarck to Hitler, France from pre revolution to the present, Rome from republic to empire, and Athens before the Peloponnesian War.

Why must we always learn the hard way? Why does it take a war that kills sixty million people and devastates the world economy before it dawns on us that the fascist and Nazi variants of socialism were and are lethal ideas? Why must tens of millions of people live for decades under brutal and culturally and economically impoverished regimes before we grasp that Marx was murderously wrong and the communist variant of socialism was and is an even more lethal idea? Why do we still have Marxist professors pouring their poison into impressionable minds?

Again why?

The terrible and distressing answer to that question? That's what people want. They want relief from life's burdens, the cost of misfortunes dumped on those allegedly better off, and a charismatic leader to seize the helm of state, steer the populous toward a mirage, seduce them into imagining that their refusal to think and provide for themselves are not the causes of interminable social discord and discontent. They'd rather unjustly accuse some minority and maligned group of predatory exploitation.

People throughout the ages have desperately wished to escape this vale of tears. They have watched loved ones die, endured every manner of tragedy, disease, war, loss, natural disaster, disappointment and grief, and cried out for some solace, some escape, some place better than this brutal world. To concoct that solace people invented history's innumerable gods, imagined Gardens of Eden and made Faustian bargains with political demagogues in desperate yearning to make that dream real. Grief and desperation reify myth. As traditional theistic religion has gradually declined, people increasingly depend on parental government to provide the same benefits and vote for deceitful candidates who promise to give it to them. Statism in the form of socialism in its many guises is a perennial mirage with all the characteristics of a replacement religion.

Democracies fail because people vote for the impossible. They want a parental government to absolve them of the impositions, cruelties and inequalities of reality. But Nature does not conform to fantasies. People are manifestly unequal in many ways and must all struggle as best they can against sickness, loss, grief and every manner of impediment. No one lacks troubles. Some face their troubles armed with greater resources and abilities than others have to face theirs. This strikes many as unfair. Is it? Why?

All attempts to forcefully level the playing field and impose by legislation some mirage of social justice have only brought additional woe and a variant of injustice not readily admitted, that is, burdening (or enviously destroying as under communism) the only people capable of gradually mitigating the ever present front of misery.

Too many people demand a free life and cry, "compensate me for the consequences of my own folly." Nature declines to cooperate.

The rise of the despot that we are encouraging on our present course must find "enemies of the people," a favorite deceit among his predecessors to explain the widespread tumult of the society for which he pretends to have the remedy, typically wholesale murder. He need not look far. People provide that service quite well themselves. Clearly we are doing this to ourselves. Walt Kelly said it best, "We have met the enemy and he is us."

Most will now add, "Let me forget this message immediately after reading it."

A welfare statist sees democracy being destroyed by everyone except the one grinning out from the mirror. Such people fool themselves with the delusion that their noble political ideal has always been brought down in the past by deceitful leaders and despots. They refuse to acknowledge that socialism in whatever form it appears from mild welfare state to totalitarianism is intrinsically unjust and anti human. Exactly what cost in time, tears and corpses it will take for people to finally let go of that delusion I do not know.

When has life not been difficult? Why do we owe one another compensation for that universal difficulty? Does not everyone have to face trials?

Now ask what politicians and demagogues get out of this game. With honest intentions?

How many more years must we endure interminable variations of upheaval before people finally get it into their heads that life cannot be free, that no one is entitled to involuntary compensation for whatever misfortunes life brings, that all does not belong to all, that the rich and the industrious do not impoverish the poor and have no moral obligation to support anyone they choose not to, and that some as yet untried variant of socialism will not and cannot work. How many more Chavezes and Castros now armed with nuclear and pathogenic bombs is it going to take?

A simple and honest rule of life: We must play as best we can the genetic and nurturing hand we are dealt however unfair that might at first impact us. Our definition of justice does not concord with Nature's perpetual arms race that we do not happen to like, but which has evolved over countless epochs to bring us to our present level of intellectual and moral confusion. We defy that progression on our peril. No misfortune no matter how debilitating entitles anyone to compensation from anyone else other than a volunteer or the individual, if any, who caused the misfortune. If such does not exist or is beyond appeal, then the victim's only recourse is to fall back on self resources however meager. A cruel injustice? Yes, according to human wishes, but no because the well-practiced alternative has guaranteed the endless cycle described at the beginning of this commentary and elaborated in this book.

Autocrats and political creatures do not have unlimited moral authority to tax the public and squander the proceeds on their demagogic fantasies and moral presumptions. They have been among the principal perpetuators of the cycles of woe. What do politicians do except argue with one another about how to rule other people's lives, control better minds, spend other people's money and dream up schemes to stay in office? The federal government's unlimited power to tax, spend and print money is a many times proven recipe for the catastrophe toward which we plunge.

The inescapable tap root of all human-caused woe: We have not evolved sufficient self awareness to understand fully why we do what we do, think what we do or believe what we believe. We instead invent self comforting but spurious explanations for those inclinations, behaviors and choices that grow out of emotional and wishful soil.

I think every intelligent person should place a single three-word question above all others: *What is True?* I define truth as what is *really* true, not what I would like to be true, not what feels good to be true, not what some alleged "holy" book claims to be true, not what any number of authorities assert as true, and not what some religious, political or academic guru pontificates. An honest quest for truth rejects the cynic's contempt for the effort as an illusion, but acknowledges our woeful predilection for feel-good answers while striving toward that eternally unreachable goal with courage, dedication and perseverance. Every human being faces a lifelong obligation to pursue truth, a quest that cannot be fulfilled in a hundred lifetimes, and not strive to impose one's own version of it on everyone else. Beliefs do not guarantee truth no matter how fervently believed. No one holds the patent on truth and those who claim to hold it are furthest from it. If anyone searches for truth within the borders of an unquestioned doctrine, be it theistic, political or personal (beliefs about one's self), he or she will never discover it.

If our self-understanding fails to keep pace with our technological progress, we will regress into children armed with extremely destructive devices and the immaturity to employ them like kids playing with loaded guns.

We should not primarily focus our inquiries on the errors of some particular philosophy such as one of the variants of a political or theistic doctrine, but toward discovering the genetic, nurturing, cultural and psychological factors that cause an individual to resonate with and be drawn to that mode of thought. Focus not on exposing the nonsense inherent in some unliked ism, but rather the cause, rooted in childhood experiences, of why people think that way.

A philosophy exposes its errors by its intolerance of other modes of thought, justifiable only when the criticized mode of thought is violent or has achieved despotism. The obligation to discover ever elusive truth must fall on all of us. We must accept that obligation with measures of humility, honesty and awareness of how easily emotion-charged preferences seduce our respect for evidence-based judgments.

What is the purpose of life? Why do people so often ask themselves this question as if it were some deep mystery? The answer lies within each of us and all around us. Hold and love a spouse. Bring happy children into the world. Develop a skill that others will value. Create. Be productive and contributing. Leave the world a bit better for you having passed through it. Clichés? Yes, but they have lost none of their relevance. Do not through your voting power demand that a successful few assume the burdens of and compensate for the losses in other individual lives.

Picture evolution as a continuum from protozoan to human genius. Then extrapolate that beyond our present peak. Do you see a teleological endpoint? There can never be one unless we ourselves arrest the process.

Now picture an infinite and eternal universe in which ever evolving humans venture, explore, discover, create, love and wonder. Add to that our species continuously striving for individual autonomy, self fulfillment and acceptance of personal responsibility for support of self, family, loved ones and one's own triumphs, tragedies, successes, afflictions and setbacks.

Isn't this image so much more profoundly edifying, exciting, momentous and transcendent than endlessly and tediously squabbling about which political party has a firm grip on truth and justice when they are all light years from it, or anguishing about some tyrant's dogma threatening to rule the world? We are a long way from reifying this image, but shouldn't it be the goal toward which humanity strives instead of the mendacious, parasitical and larcenous world in which we currently decline?

OUR DECLINING SOCIETY

A CHILD WHO LEARNS NO SENSE OF RESPONSIBILITY, even so simple a discipline as cleaning his room, will develop no sense of self efficacy either. If he is not responsible for anything, how can he develop a conviction that he controls the direction of his life? And will this not in the later adult engender defeat and resignation among the timid, and anger and hostility among the aggressive?

As accepted social principles shift slowly from individual to collective responsibility, everyone will be looking to everyone else for moral direction. The society must inevitably grow more authoritarian because the government, particularly one central government, must act as agent of that collective responsibility and fill the vacuum created by the many individual resignations. Authoritarianism further encourages hostility and rebellion particularly among those who think poorly, cannot understand the social complexities in which they are immersed, and live at the level of whims driven by feelings.

No society can be philosophically monolithic, not even so focused a regime as Nazi Germany or Soviet Russia. A society can be seen as immersed in and defined by a cloud of ideas, diffuse but with a central core that gives the society a universally recognized identity. At the outer edges of this cloud live the misfits, the disaffected, the neurotic and the rebellious who constantly clash with reality or with the body of dominant ideas that form the animating nucleus of the cloud.

A bright self-respecting person raised and steeped in the culture of let's say a Soviet Union or a United States drifting from its original defining principles, may well feel disaffected and imagine that the cloud of ideas that prevail in his society convey the source of his discontent. He might lack the ability to define the disaffection with specifics clear enough to focus his protest on any particular issue. Or his discontent might arise from some unacknowledged distant past injustice done to him personally that has nothing to do with his society. So his fight, if he fights at all, assumes diffuse forms of him against all. He generates sparks around the perimeter of his society's cloud of ideas that erupt in explosions of anger and frustration and take the forms of a kid with a gun in a high school, a postal worker taking it out on uncomprehending work-place authorities charged with upholding the rules, a deranged chemistry tinkerer blowing up a federal building in Oklahoma, or the much more recent spate of terrorist horrors.

Consider the cloud of ideas defined at its center by the thoughts, writings and comportments of Locke, Jefferson, Franklin, Washington, Madison, Thomas Paine and Sam Adams, all except Locke incredibly existing at the same time and in the same place. Contrast this with the ideas promulgated by our recent presidents and numerous Americans who embrace their doctrines. A president like Biden, Trump or Obama would no more have been possible at the founding of this country than someone like Washington, Jefferson or Madison could be elected in the 21st Century. Clearly a philosophical shift has taken place, one not explainable by the avarice so often cited as the source of our national sickness. Capitalism embodied in greedy bankers, heartless businesspeople and reactionary conservatives, the putative causes of our current malaise, were also raised in a society that emphasizes collective responsibility and central authority, one that distrusts, even disparages, individual initiative, business and industry.

Who promulgates the ideas that drive our present culture? And from where do these ideas come? To the first question, principally the American education establishment, K through PhD, and the news media, to my mind public enemy numbers one and two and subjects of later essays.

To the second question we would have to go back to the beginning of civilization, to our very nature, and to a fundamental set of questions: Are we primarily social creatures or individuals? If both, where is the boundary between? What are our obligations to others? What is good? How can we know what is good? How can we be sure we are doing good? As societies, how do we structure ourselves? How do we determine the balance between the needed order of society and the equally needed creative freedom of the individual? What is freedom and how does it differ from licentiousness or hedonism?

Prior to the Greeks these questions were answered by priestly mysticism coupled to political force. In most societies since, those two acting in concert have typically dealt harshly with social malcontents. In contemporary societies the priest has been replaced by the government "expert," an individual selected because he or she most adroitly rationalizes current desired policy. It is that current policy and its philosophical underpinnings that distinguish the United States of today from that orphaned nation of the same name born so many years ago in a radically different world. What happened?

Look not to a long sequence of events but to an evolution of ideas. Since I cannot go back to the beginning of time, I arbitrarily point to a cataclysmic event that in relatively modern times accelerated the slide into the cloud of ideas that presently envelopes us. That event was the French Revolution that began in 1789 in which for the first time leftist, that is, socialist, principles advanced, if that's the right word, into statutes. Indeed, the philosophical battleground of our time could be symbolized in the sharp contrast between the nearly concurrent American and French Revolutions. The first was largely definable by the individual seeking freedom from authority, the second by the individual induced to submerge into the collective.

Since the birth of our country, the people of this unprecedented great nation have gradually recoiled from the risks attendant to accepting individual responsibility and instead adopted the ideas that fired the French Revolution. The process accelerated after the American Civil War and much more so since the election of Franklin Roosevelt, an election that could not have happened unless the ideas that he represented had not long since found their way into the minds of a majority of voters.

If the worldwide adoption of collectivist ideas has not been the principal cause of the seminal philosophical shift of our time, how would one explain the rise of Stalin, Hitler, Mao, Mussolini, Pol Pot and dozens of lesser thugs all in the same century and all preaching minor variations of the same doctrine? And what institutions in the contemporary United States teach a diluted and compromised form of this same doctrine? And what has been and will be the result of this shift? Widespread belief in a destructive idea converts the ludicrous into the tragic.

If the men who fought the Revolutionary War could have foreseen what this nation has become, they would have thrown away their muskets and kissed King George. We have clearly betrayed them.

When I have watched or read a Shakespeare drama, listened to a Mozart symphony, a Beethoven concerto, a Schubert sonata, or gazed in wonder at Michelangelo's David in Florence or Raphael and Bernini in Rome, tears came forth unbidden only to retreat following a sad reflection on what our morally inverted world has offered in place of these celestial masters. What a disheartening descent from the pinnacles of accomplishment of which humans are capable.

My recollection elicited the scene with Hamlet upbraiding his mother when he compared the image of his father to that of his uncle, a Hyperion to a "mildew'd ear"[1], in other words the noble to the base, the majesty of Everest to the lifeless desiccation of a desert.

Our political trend follows a similar steep decline. Down to what depth we must wonder. Compare the honor, courage and enlightenment of the men who founded this nation to those who have in recent decades reached the heights of influence and power. Deceit has upstaged honor. The demagogue has eclipsed the statesman. The comparison cannot help but evoke sadness. We must now seize Churchill's inspiration to fight on even in the dark absence of hope because honorable men cannot act otherwise. In our present political conflict, perhaps the barbarians will win. It won't be the first time.

When the reigning ideology demands that the government solve all problems and succor all misfortunes, countless demagogues rise like miasma from a swamp, each armed with a plan to leash people to his design and march us all in blissful unity in pursuit of his forever receding fantasy on a trail of tears and blood.

Suppose that I were asked by a political office candidate or holder what he or she could do to advance the cause of freedom and improve the American economy.

I would answer, "Get out of politics and create, invent, or produce something that people need and want. Then spend your own money and time to help alleviate the innumerable problems that torment and shorten our lives. You will find no shortage of causes on which to devote your 'generosity.'

"In the capacity as a politician your question is dishonest. The answer you want would promote the very harmful trend for which your question ostensibly seeks a remedy. The government solution, which you evidently seek, *is* a major part of the problem. You want some grand program with your name on it that you can establish and operate with other people's money and create yet another government department so you can feel big hearted, morally superior and hold on to your office."

When the Virginia politician, democrat Congresswoman Abigail Spanberger, told her listeners: "We need to not ever use the word 'socialist' or 'socialism' ever again." she was exhorting them to lie (November 2020). Her admonition evokes the old joke about how to identify a duck: if it looks like a duck, quacks like a duck, swims like a duck and walks like a duck, it most probably is a duck. If someone talks like a socialist, writes like a socialist and votes like a socialist, avoiding the conclusion that said person is a socialist colludes with deceit.

Spanberger's prevarication exposed the hypocrisy of a political party that never ceases to remind us that it represents the people and values democracy, but must hide its true intentions behind a giant lie for fear of losing votes.

The near universal fears that preclude choosing honorable political leaders also sabotage honest searches for truth. We fear and detest the suffering, perceived injustices and brevity of life. We want to mitigate that pain and have called upon our gods and now the State to bring that relief. Unfortunately the first is a delusion and the second a fraud. Nevertheless we keep trying the same formulae and in the trying we perpetuate our sentence of incarceration in a prison of fantasy hope.

Incremental statism would be a good label for the present trend in the U.S. The rolling snowball of the last two centuries has grown into an avalanche. The government is pouring wealth down unproductive holes faster than productive people can generate it. That process can have only one outcome, economic ruin. This is simple arithmetic, not inscrutable political philosophy.

Socialism in whatever guise it appears from murderous communism and fascism to much milder welfare statism is counter-natural and inherently unjust. When people strive in whatever endeavor they have chosen in accordance with their ability and ambition, the process naturally results in a hierarchy of competence, achievement and wealth, envy from socialist minds and ambrosia for demagogues.

I have struggled to locate a balance point between individual autonomy, responsibility and efficacy versus individual suffering, incapacities and unfeigned helplessness. Further, to what extent are the more able *obliged* to compensate the less able? I resolved both questions by heavily favoring individual autonomy and leaving charity to voluntary choice. I base that conclusion not on denial of widespread undeserved suffering to which we all are subject, but the threat posed by statutory compassion, an ominous oxymoron I inveterately distrust, that sets us on a slippery slide toward a precipice of no return.

Regarding politics, my greatest fear is of the relentless expansion of government authority[2], intrusion and expense, in a word, *statism,* which should be our most worrisome contemporary threat. There is hardly a single historic example of big government being healthy for people. I know of none but leave the question open as a possibility.

Picture a huge broken sewer pipe spewing massive amounts of pollution into a river. Downstream property owners, alarmed by the disaster, lack the resources to remediate the situation and the understanding of how such an awful breach of normalcy could have happened. They do what they can within their capacities, but their efforts are ludicrously inadequate to stem the tide of contamination.

See this as a metaphor for our massively corrupted politics.

It has taken a few generations for a very few people to finally grasp the magnitude of the stark evil that has crept into and grasped this country by the throat, much less do they know what to do about it.

What values do politicians bring into the world that can be placed on the tray of a balance scale with the opposing tray loaded with the harm they bring? The tray holding the harms sinks to its limit with little or nothing to counterbalance it. A reading of history reveals no hopeful counter examples. Politics is among the least useful professions although its practitioners delude themselves and most of the rest of the population into believing the contrary. What exactly do they do other than compete with one another dreaming up schemes to spend other people's money, pass laws no one needs, flit about their constituent territory promising benefits, preaching the superiority of their worldview, heaping scorn on the opposition, and convincing themselves and the voters of the great need for their wisdom? For what do we need these people?

Instead of what they should be doing, preserving freedom and protecting citizens from human predators including themselves, Congress has shirked the single law-making responsibility assigned to it by the Constitution by empowering myriad regulatory agencies to create rules with all the force of law but answerable to no one. Delegating responsibility can only expand the abuses of which Congress is already guilty but leaves its members free to devote their expensive time constructing their ideal parental government that fosters dependent, irresponsible and compliant voters. In their capacity as members of Congress, they create little of value to the nation, yet delude themselves and most of their constituents with presumptions of moral superiority that permit them to instruct other people about how they should conduct their lives and on what they must devote their resources. At least they have provided us with good examples of hubris.

We should respect the law. But then those entrusted with the task must enact respectable laws that invite compliance. Is that what we see happening?

Contempt of Congress has been amply justified by the dereliction of its members past and present. The more that citizens are treated like dependent children, the more they behave like ineffectually grousing dependent children who vote for candidates who promise benefits with other people's money. Political types want the glory of accomplishment but not the personal risk, a dilemma resolved with money confiscated from taxpayers. Then they take credit for the project. Did John Kennedy or his money send us to the moon or just grandstand a few inspiring words with the magic word *we*?

Presidential executive orders and judge-made law also carry the force of law. Why these travesties were not declared unconstitutional decades ago would make a revealing study in malfeasance. A clearer violation of Article 1, Section 1, would be difficult to cite.

All three branches of government have become models of self-serving irresponsibility.

Religious conservatives blame the decline of our country on the drift away from God and Constitution, blithely unaware that science and psychology have so eroded belief in God that religion no longer holds any intellectual force in the world. The philosophical understandings that inspired the drafting of the Constitution have been lost and religious conservatives cry for rededication to a document they do not understand.

"Liberals" blame our decline on the great disparity of wealth and preach the egalitarian fantasy that gets them elected while they vilify the only people capable of reversing that decline.

We must stop blaming government for the slow disintegration of our freedom. We are doing this to ourselves. Voters throughout the world have consistently shown that they want their nanny states. If American voters want their nanny state with all of its "free" benefits, then big, ugly, snoopy, rule-choked and ruinously expensive government inescapably comes with the package. Government parentalism is expensive, intrusive and diminishes self-reliant adults to supplicating children. Such a demoralizing trend can only end where democracies have always ended, in autocracy. Athens before Pericles and Republican Rome furnish the best examples of the process and we badly fool ourselves when we believe that we have advanced sufficiently in the last two millennia to preclude it happening again here. Democrats and republicans hurling insults and blame at one another for our fiscal mess and calling one another liars (both are correct) is grossly dishonest and self-exonerating. Neither side in our political burlesque has the slightest clue to the cause of the sickness for which they prescribe exacerbating remedies. Both groups insist that the government must assume the role of a parent and make sure that we do not fall when we stumble. We have little cause to grumble when the bills arrive at the door while the government grows like an invading cancer.

When the disintegration of the unprecedented American way of life finally reaches its hellish climax, American voters will have only themselves to blame, which of course they will not do. Socialism always needs some group to blame for the doctrine's endemic failures.

At root our political problems are not political nor our social conflicts sociological. They will not therefore be resolved by politicians, sociologists or some political writer. They are psychological and rooted in the capabilities of the mind and how we think or not. They will be solved, if at all, by the people who study the brain, the mind, or work with patients struggling with emotional and cognitive confusion.

It matters not what anyone's political leanings are or what direction anyone thinks the country should be heading. We cannot arrive there by piling up debt, then paying it off by printing money.

Are we looking for our model among Europe's welfare states? They are all broke and broke for the same reason we are. Voters want to suck on a government nipple and insist that "the rich" pay the bills. And when "the rich" are bled white or desperately try to escape or hide their money from the tax collector as in Southern Europe, what then? Look for scapegoats: the few remaining less rich, the big corporations (if any), the greedy capitalists (they can be invented), the narrow-minded republicans, the profligate democrats, anything and anyone except the one glaring out from the mirror.

Why is it a crime to be rich and evil to pursue profit? Wealth should be both inspiration and aspiration.

You cannot be dependent and free at the same time. You cannot be a child and a self-determining adult at the same time. The fact that someone has wealth that you lack entitles you to nothing except to apply whatever resources you possess to earn wealth yourself. Your inability or unwillingness to be self-dependent confers no entitlement.

On whom are we to blame the erosion of freedom and the bloating of government when voters consistently chose candidates who promise to expand the nanny state? You cannot be free and have a free life. Not even a child enjoys that privilege.

The more that people depend on the government to rescue them from the consequences of their failures to act effectively in their own interests, the more that they will demand expansion of that function, and the more that the government will grow more intrusive, authoritarian and expensive. Is this not what continues to choke us?

If this world is ever to get better, only one class of people are capable of bringing that about: the intelligent, inventive, rational, independent, self-knowledgeable and productive.

The solution to our political problems is most likely that which we find most repellant. Therefore, the solution will most likely continue to elude us.

We are engaged in a deadly race between self-knowledge and self-destruction. If good fails to triumph over the current torments in our world, then evil surely will.

Statists do not want people to solve their own problems. They do not want anyone to be independent. Social and political problems are grist for the statist mill. Their goal is not to solve problems but interminably pretend to address them from within an authoritarian office that assures security, perks and delusions of moral superiority. Comfortably entrenched in bureaucratic anonymity, they maneuver to bankrupt and corrupt the morals of whatever remains of the society that values individual freedom, initiative and responsibility, the better to replace it with one ruled by their own kind. Statists love political problems so much that they even invent them.

I describe here only one type of statist. Still worse are the much more visible born-to-rule types who contend with whatever foul means to reach the top of the power pyramid, the ones compelled by some yet unexplained psychopathology to always be in control. Putin and Xi provide good contemporary examples.

Imagine all the bold, new and exciting programs the statists can initiate with other people's money and little more persuasion than the magic word *we*. They enjoy public applause and authoritative office but endure none of the risk, expense or hard work. What a hell of a racket. Small wonder why they claim to love politics and democracy so much.

Our perennial tug-of-war is not between left and right, democrat and republican, liberal and conservative, but an endless struggle between individual responsibility and collective larceny.

NOTES

1   Act 3, Scene 4
2   The subject of the cover story in *The Economist*, November 20-26, 2021.

THE COLLECTIVIST MIND

RECALL FOR A MOMENT a familiar exhortation, "Ask not what your country can do for you; ask what you can do for your country."[1] I have never been an admirer of Mr. Kennedy, his canonized memory or that hackneyed quotation that has come to represent his "charismatic leadership." Better if he had said, and sincerely meant as a moral principle and not grandstanding pretentiousness, "Ask not what your country can do for you, but what you can do for yourself unseduced by some demagogue's hypocritical concern for your welfare."

Another one from him, "We choose to go to the moon. We chose to go to the moon. We choose to go to the moon in this decade and do the other things not because they are easy, but because they are hard."[2]

His invocation of the royal *we* was sufficient to galvanize the nation into funding an extravagantly expensive undertaking to land a man on the moon, an undeniably exciting project in which I played an insignificant off-stage role.[3]

It was "hard" for whom? Certainly not for him. His contributions amounted to vocalizing a kingly wish to which most people nodded compliance and that relegated feeble protests to the closet. He left behind a clichéd quotation that sustained the innumerable contributors who really did work very hard to realize that world-mesmerizing achievement.

Mr. Kennedy can serve here as a paradigm of the kind of political leadership that we must dethrone as one of the costs of our transition from species adolescence to individual self-actuating maturity. The project that he initiated was only the most spectacular of the many "bold new programs" that have marked our nation's "progress" toward the statists' goal of reducing us all to subjects under the unchallengeable authority of a clique of sycophants ruled by a party "secretary," precisely the goal toward which we must *not* advance.

How much more self-satisfying to the statist, contemptuous of the slow risky entrepreneurial progress of wealth accumulation, is taxing and spending other people's money in riskless pursuit of their leader's fantasies of national goals and public adulation.

We should instead applaud the courage of the plodding individuals who risk their own comparatively modest resources in pursuit of wealth, security and pride of accomplishment, the same process that provides wealth for the statists to tax, an imposition best described as ignominious theft rationalized as justice. Entrepreneurial independence stands out like a bullseye for the statists' scorn because it exposes their aversion to risking their own money and unimpressive talents.

When then President Obama said, "You didn't build that," (see below), his detractors gleefully seized the comment out of context as proof that he was a statist through and through.

His supporters claimed, I think correctly, that he referred to the help businesspeople and others receive from government funded infrastructure like highways, bridges, water and electrical distribution systems and the internet. Add to those the interstate highway system, national forests and parks, dams, levies, flood control plus many other benefits including the military and police, all of which enormously benefit the public and, as he pointed out, businesses depend on to make a profit. It is difficult to see how these benefits could have come about without eminent domain and public funding. In that sense Mr. Obama was right.

During my walk one morning along the beautiful, functional and essential seawall in Carlsbad, California, I thought of Obama's words. That sea wall was built in the 1980s under the direction of and funded by the California Department of Beaches and Harbors, that is, by California taxpayers.

The seawall prevents or greatly reduces erosion of the loose soil bluffs that separate the roadway above from the beach below. The concrete seawall and other erosion mitigation projects now separate the two and, consistent with Obama's words, permit businesses to operate on ground that was, pre-sea-wall, vulnerable to sliding down to the beach. Other examples dot the coast.

From Wikipedia (emphasis in the original):

On July 13, 2012, during a campaign swing through Virginia, Obama stopped in Roanoke to speak to supporters. In his remarks Obama noted that while he was willing to cut government waste, he would not gut investments that grow the economy or give tax breaks to millionaires like himself or Mitt Romney. Obama went on to say that rich people did not get rich solely due to their own talent and hard work, but that, to varying degrees, they owe some of their success to good fortune and the contributions of government. Obama said in this context:

"There are a lot of wealthy, successful Americans who agree with me – because they want to give something back. They know they didn't – look, if you've been successful, you didn't get there on your own. You didn't get there on your own. I'm always struck by people who think, well, it must be because I was just so smart. There are a lot of smart people out there. It must be because I worked harder than everybody else. Let me tell you something – there are a whole bunch of hardworking people out there. (Applause.)

"If you were successful, somebody along the line gave you some help. There was a great teacher somewhere in your life. Somebody helped to create this unbelievable American system that we have that allowed you to thrive. Somebody invested in roads and bridges--if you've got a business, **you didn't build that**. Somebody else made that happen. The Internet didn't get invented on its own. Government research created the Internet so that all the companies could make money off the Internet.

"The point is, is that when we succeed, we succeed because of our individual initiative, but also because we do things together. There are some things, just like fighting fires, we don't do on our own. I mean, imagine if everybody had their own fire service. That would be a hard way to organize fighting fires."

Obama then cited the funding of the G.I. Bill, the creation of the middle class, the construction of the Golden Gate Bridge and Hoover Dam, creation of the Internet, and landing on the moon as examples of what he was talking about.

Each of us is at once an individual and a member of various collectives. I think that Mr. Obama, as is his predilection, placed much emphasis on collective efforts and benefits, and little to none on uncommon individual initiative and intrepid willingness to risk failure in pursuit of goals.

An individual cannot be granted license to follow whatever whims drive him or her, nor should the collective — in practice government authority acting through numerous agencies — run rough shod over individual initiative. So where do we build a wall on the slippery slope between individual and collective enterprise? The relative success and public good when each has been emphasized at different times and places points toward an ambiguous answer.

Isaac Newton famously declared perhaps with false modesty, "If I have seen further than others, it is by standing upon the shoulders of giants." True, the small increments of discovery and innovation that gave Newton those giant shoulders to stand on were brought to him by innumerable predecessors.

The collective mind argument can easily reach and has reached the absurd conclusion that if Beethoven had not composed his incomparable

Ninth Symphony, someone else would have. The symphony was "in the air" so to speak. The world was "ripe" for it, so goes the argument.

True, notes, musical harmony, structure and rules had already been laid down previously to enable Beethoven to create that magnificent monument to genius.

But Newton and Beethoven produced unparalleled works that could not have been created by lesser minds in their respective times, if ever. No one of comparable stature has arisen since the deaths of those two except perhaps Einstein who came close to Newton. No one has come close to Beethoven since his death.

I detect in the collective mind argument something sinister like envy. Why the great emphasis, especially in today's world, on collective accomplishment? Obama's "You didn't build that" is a case in point. True, most every discovery or innovation rests on prior efforts by others. But isn't the collective mind argument no more than an envious attempt to share the glory or diminish genius?

The excessive emphasis that most politicians place on collective projects and alleged social improvements raises the suspicion that they do not want independent citizens. They want you to depend on them, the more the better. They must rationalize their presumptuous self-value.

Every single improvement in anything, major or tiny, was brought into the world by some *one*. The argument that if Smith did not do it, Jones would have, erodes to a sour grapes whimper by the inescapable fact that Smith did it and Jones did not think of it, saw no need, did not try, failed the attempt or arrived too late. Too bad, Mr. Jones, that's how priority works, and you deserve no recognition equal to Smith's.

NOTES

1   From President Kennedy's inaugural address, January 20, 1961.
2   From his speech at Rice University, September 12, 1962 reputedly written by Ted Sorensen.
3   The United States spent $28 billion to land men on the Moon between 1960 and 1973, or approximately $280 billion when adjusted for inflation [in 2020]. — The Planetary Society

RIGHTS

*R*IGHTS has become the most overused and misunderstood word in political discourse.

Consider a statement familiar to many Americans: (capitalizations in the original):

> WE hold these Truths to be self-evident, that all Men are created equal, that they are endowed by their Creator with certain inalienable Rights, that among these are Life, Liberty, and the Pursuit of Happiness …

Much as I revere Thomas Jefferson, his statement confronts me with a couple of troubling obstacles not easily ignored.

One, my rejection of the concept of a presumably divine Creator yanks the foundation from under the statement and leaves it insecurely resting on an opinion, a venerable opinion to be sure, but still an opinion.

Second, if *Nature* replaces *Creator*, then when and by what means were our rights secured? Does the terminal cancer victim have a right to life and liberty? Who or what will guarantee it?

Do animals have natural, that is, Nature endowed, rights? Does the lion respect the impala's right to life, liberty and the pursuit of happiness? Does the neighbor's cat respect the rights of the birds that come and go in my back yard?

Are we not animals? Humans evolved from a remote ancestor that we share with other great ape primates, unarguably an animal. When during the six million years or so since that creature lived did our ancestors acquire natural rights? From whom? By what means? The short answer: they didn't. We have no inalienable rights endowed by any entity or thing other than ourselves and that's a very unreliable endower.

"Ah!" declares the collectivist. "We give rights to ourselves through the democratic process."

Oh, really? We can't seem to agree on what these rights might be, and they proliferate like mosquitos. Improvidently multiplying rights like printing dollars by the trillion erodes the value of each. Voters have proven capable of rationalizing their rights to the treasury to compensate themselves for the intrinsic burdens and expenses of life with their political representatives eager to accommodate. The democratic process elected Hitler and Hugo Chavez and brought catastrophe to Germany and Venezuela. The democratic process elects republicans (Trump a notable exception) that the lefties hate, and elects democrats that the righties hate. Lenin and Castro were not elected at all but rose to power on huge waves of popular savior worship in two variants of the democratic process. The great majority seems to love democracy until they don't like the results it brings.

My first criticism of an often cited idea of basing individual rights on human nature derives from the fact that human nature is not a singularity. The nature of geniuses differs profoundly from that of fools, similarly that of an individualist from a collectivist, and men from women. I strongly suspect that the often contentious world views within each of the noted pairs reach much greater depths than mere philosophical disagreements. To a significant degree they are genetic, that is, built-in fundamentals of irreconcilable personalities. That makes their differing views of reality effects of their different human natures.

Secondly, human nature is not yet defined with sufficient precision to serve as a firm foundation for any vital principle such as rights. Common experience often hints of a reality that lies beyond our present knowledge.

We do not know the cause of cancer and cannot reverse vascular disease or mental illness, our worse scourges, or for that matter the common cold. Then by what arrogance do we presume greater certainties in our political doctrines or definitions of our nature than those offered by our hard sciences and medicine both of which rest on far firmer ground? The left contests with the right, liberal with conservative, and collectivist with individualist in endless tedious arguments that presume understandings absurdly inadequate to the subject over which the antagonists presume certainty.

Thirdly, I see no reason to limit rights to individuals. A nation of individuals has a right to be protected from foreign invasion, or a neighborhood of individuals protected from criminals.

Fourthly, many argue that the foundation of individual rights rests on declaring man a rational animal. We can easily see that rationality, like intelligence, manifests itself in a continuum, not an all or nothing phenomenon. The precious few rational people among us, that is, those who respect reason and un-cherry-picked evidence and do not bond themselves to some unquestioned dogma, flounder in a sea of overwhelming irrationality. A fool is intrinsically irrational, that is, not irrational from choice but beyond his nature and evidently not that exceptional. A presumption of man's rationality, therefore, sets such vital principles as human rights on quicksand.

When Jefferson wrote the words, "...endowed by our creator with..." he faced no risk of being misunderstood. Few atheists and fewer still with influence were around in 1776 to protest his assumption of the existence of a creator although he was not religious. If he had instead written, "... endowed by our human nature with...", he would at the very least have evoked a few raised eyebrows and questions like, "what exactly do you mean, Thomas?" Now 246 years later we grapple with the same imprecision.

We do not know ourselves very well, why we think what we do, believe what we do, choose the philosophy that we do and behave as we do. Such mental and behavioral preferences or patterns find their common root in differing native intelligences, genetic endowments of whatever kind, childhood nurturing, cultural influences, and finally the choices we make all of which are heavily influenced by the noted factors. None of this is understood very well and in many, if not most people, not even acknowledged as personality-determining influences. Given such presently insurmountable obstacles, how can anyone uncontroversially define human nature as a secure foundation of rights?

I must conclude from all this that we really do not have any inalienable rights, naturally endowed or otherwise, and won't have until we can with much greater clarity and assurance discover the fundamentals, if any, that divide humankind from other animals that we pet, abuse, kill and eat at our pleasure.

As an alternative to this grim conclusion, I return to a principle earlier rejected: we give rights to ourselves through the democratic process. The more rational among us must acknowledge the treachery and political menace that loom like specters over that declaration. At this time in our glacial progress of enlightenment, do we really have another choice?

Contrary to initial appearances I am not a sophist, deconstructionist or relativist who cynically dismisses the search for truth as an impossible illusion or worse yet, declares reality itself an illusion. Reality and truth exist independent of our puerile interpretations. We cannot, must not, absolve ourselves from their pursuit, but doggedly persist in the never ending never fulfillable quest for what is true.

Everyone claims a hold on truth usually embodied in their respective beliefs. The missing principle in the endlessly contentious efforts to impose one's version of the truth on everyone else is respect for the means we have to discover it. The method of science discovery has been developed specifically as an attempt to overcome our predilection for feel-good answers. It is not of course fool proof, meaning safe from fools, but all we have.

Beliefs do not guarantee truth no matter how fervently believed. Truth must never be permitted to become an expedient to be piously invoked when it advances the cause, and ignored, distorted or denied when not. An individual's lifelong pursuit of real rather than presumed truth is nothing less than a moral obligation. Once that quest has reached a comfortable consensus, we can with much greater assurance return to the definition and enumeration of rights.

A BRIEF LOOK AT PROGRESS

S OME FORM OF COLLECTIVISM has structured communities since the
dawn of humanity. Pleistocene tribal communities consisted of extended
families wherein everyone knew one another, moved about as nomadic hunt-
er-gatherers, accumulated little or nothing, struggled for survival just barely
within the boundary of subsistence and lived short brutal lives.

Much later people left us written records. We can now read of the begin-
nings of fixed settlements based on agriculture in Sumer (in Mesopotamia),
Egypt, Assyria and other very early civilizations. The government in the
person of the King or Pharaoh owned everything and everyone worked for
the common good as directed by the autocrat and his ministers and priests.

Still later, particularly in Greece and Rome, we read about artisans who
applied their skills in simple manufacturing and artwork; professional people
offering valued services like medicine, architecture and teaching; traders
who accepted great risks in a dangerous world moving goods and foodstuffs
across distant borders and unpredictable seas; and great numbers of slaves
who provided much of the unpleasant physical labor. Other than the slaves,
a universally accepted reality at that time, these contributing people, always
a small minority in the population, earned their way through life more or
less independent of their rulers, the orbiting aristocracy, the priestly class,
the military, and an abundance of parasitical drones. They were unwittingly
building the rough foundations of entrepreneurial enterprise that would later
enrich first the West and later the entire world.

History of the succeeding centuries weeps and bleeds with the wars, despotism, larceny and corruption of pompous rulers, their relatives and sycophants, but with little appreciation, much less praise, afforded to the thinkers, innovators, artisans and builders who lived under the heels of that authority while creating the wealth that funded regal arrogance and extravagance.

We finally come to three contrasting world-altering revolutions, two of them violent, all occurring during or beginning in the 18th century: the Industrial in Britain, the American and the French. The American Revolution for the first time in history inverted the hierarchy of authority, at last elevating individuals to a position of authority over their government, and from where individuals could largely determine the courses of their own lives. The experiment survived pretty much intact for about a century and resulted in an astounding explosion of invention, entrepreneurial profusion and multiplication of wealth never before seen.

The French Revolution, in part inspired by the American revolt with much the same rhetoric, failed its promise. It quickly turned murderous and reverted to autocracy, never to this day coming close to the promises of its early revolutionaries. The French state, like every other state in the contemporary world, extends its tendrils into every organ of society, leaving Western voters to choose among demagogues who, to keep their jobs, compete with schemes to steal from the rich in order to bribe the spuriously entitled. A parade of charlatans has been on stage in the United States since the Civil War, dramatizing a dystopian trend that has rapidly accelerated since the turn of the 20th Century.

One should conclude from reading this very brief and inadequate account that genuine progress, in sharp contrast to its much ballyhooed counterfeit, is underpinned by freedom of the individual from government authority, precisely the opposite of what is being pounded into us daily from virtually every source of information.

The progress of thought has advanced in uncountable small painful increments, each scorned, belittled, taxed and sometimes killed under the prevailing malice of much smaller minds.

We are reverting back several thousand years to a pharaonic structure promoted by today's *regressives* who delude themselves and most others by perpetrating a gigantic fraud puffed up with self flatteries like "progressive," "liberal," "avant guard," compassionate and claims that they advocate what they call "social justice," a deceit to rationalize universal larceny. If guided by a dogma, any political or social movement is confined to the compass of the dogma as if it were fastened to the end of a chain.

Must we regress to that ancient structure so loved by statists, permit the government to own everything, the politically "correct" to run the government and delude ourselves into believing that we have achieved progress?

JUSTICE

Partially excerpted from *America's Suicide*, 2nd Edition

WE LIVE IN AN UNJUST WORLD. Not unjust in the sense of the common prattle about the rich exploiting the poor, or because of Nature's capricious distribution of talent and circumstance, but because we are sacrificing the best within us to some of the worst: ambition sacrificed to envy, intelligence to mediocrity, wealth to underserved guilt, achievement to exaggerated helplessness, independence to supplication, the risk-accepting entrepreneur to the government grant, the statesman to the demagogue.

Many people reject the view of a political structure in perpetual conflict between producer and consumer, or exploiter and victim, but see the ideal society as an extended community of sharers. Each contributes what he or she can and takes what he or she needs. In this model no one exploits anybody. If the word *exploit* is stripped of its predatory tone, then everyone can be seen as exploiting everyone else as in depending on one another for mutual benefit. In the resulting model, seen in simplest terms, the Earth is home to all and all belongs to all except minor personal articles. Those most able provide the professional services and managerial skills needed by the whole community including themselves. The less able furnish the labor to make it all possible. There are no rich or poor, but an egalitarian distribution prevails where those with superior talents, abilities or circumstances compensate those who suffer with less. The resultant society functions under what people commonly refer to as social justice.

Is this a Garden of Eden fairy tale where the lion is supposed to lie down with the lamb, but people are intrinsically bad as in selfish and greedy because they can't ever seem to get it right? Or is something intrinsically wrong with the ideal?

The nature versus nurture debate that divided psychologists for so many years finally resolved itself in the obvious. Both leave a heavy stamp on our development and the relative influence of each eludes definition. But the argument survives in a kind of political twin. The now much diminished acrimony of the psychological controversy shows no sign of abating in the twin. Are we sovereign individuals or members of a collective bound together like cells in a political body? Do we pursue our own ends while paying only lip service and taxes toward community needs, or are we morally obligated to serve the commonwealth to the extent of our capacity?

Is the statement, "From each according to his ability; to each according to his need" morally superior to, "To each according to his ability, ambition and honesty?"

If you think so, why? What makes the first statement seem more just than the second other than its emotional appeal and superficial logic? Setting aside the emotional appeal and digging a bit below that superficial logic, the statement is a rationalization for universal larceny.

Does the statement carry any moral or legal legitimacy? Aside from any moral considerations, the assertion confronts us with an inherent dilemma. Abilities have limits either in individuals or collectively. Needs do not. Any individual claimant is demonstrably capable of multiplying needs without end, particularly if he has no need to pay for them. How then does the statement represent justice even in its relatively milder Western welfare state manifestation? The present ballooning of the American government has evidently overlooked these simple principles.

It would be healthier if this argument could be resolved in the obvious like its psychological counterpart, but the question of exactly where to locate the dividing line between obligations to self and loved ones and obligations to community and nation is currently ripping our country apart. It would at least be of great benefit to recognize that both apply. Then we can pursue a workable blend of the two without all the rancor that contaminates the present debate, a blend that meets *rational* public needs without bankrupting or stifling the productive people and industries who pay the bills. The current exasperating wrangling during the formation of government policy is immature reason shaking its ineffectual fist at the hegemony of emotion and myth.

Few would reject the offer of subsidized or free food, housing, education, medical care, clothing, childcare, guaranteed income and on down the bottomless litany of demagoguery.

These unfulfillable promises resonate with the same yearning that brought us history's numberless gods. But even if actually realized, would such an outcome be good for us? Is the later political mythology any more realistic than the earlier theistic one?

Conflict will always arise between people who work toward what they call progress and others who do not regard the proposed changes as progressive. The conflicts can reach insurrectional proportions when government commits its power to one side of the dispute. The favored side, confident in the righteousness of its mission, gleefully moves to entrench its reforms in law while the other side bitterly seeks to cast out the power behind the changes. In our time the conflict has focused on the ancient debate between man the social animal and man the individual. In other words, does my life belong solely to me or am I bound under some Rousseau-like social contract to State, community, society, God, or whatever? If so, to what extent am I my brother's keeper?

If you accept the concept of a social contract in the Rousseau sense, you bind yourself to a unilateral agreement that contains no definition or limit to your service. The enforcers and adjudicators of the contract -- in our case innumerable government agencies and functionaries -- may demand and expect whatever they imagine to lie within the public interest up to and including your life, for example, the military draft.

Am I my brother's keeper and if so, to what extent? If the answer is no, then the whole socialist inspired welfare state, the nanny state, or what I prefer to call the parental state, collapses. I answer the question for me alone with a provisional and cautious *yes* that heavily depends on who I consider my brother and why he is in need. This is a voluntary choice. Under no circumstances should the principle become a moral imperative extended to everyone, let alone a universal law.

If a yes answer expands to a moral imperative, then to what extent do we apply the principle? A soviet style America? All is owned by all with the government acting as distributor and caretaker? And what will be done to those who rebel against what they perceive as an injustice? Which raises the question about the definition of justice.

John Rawls (1921-2002) wrote a widely read and tendentious book that assumes from the outset that justice means what he called fairness in distributing the society's resources of which he included individual abilities and wealth and a good chunk of everything else. His book does not present an objective search for a moral foundation of justice, but a scholarly affirmation of his version of it, a version that Professor Rawls took as a given at the starting point of his argument.

An equally compelling point of view regards taking from the able and ambitious and giving to the less able and/or ambitious, minus steep handling charges, is a rank *in*justice. That viewpoint confines the word *fairness* to human interactions, not natural events. Accordingly, the concept of fairness does not apply to personal misfortunes arising from accident of birth or acts of Nature, and good fortune has no moral obligation to compensate bad, only a legal one at present.

I quote Rawls at some length because his statements drive to the heart of the argument that we are *obligated* to share our personal abilities and achievements with those less fortunate:

> First we may observe that the difference principle gives some weight
> to the considerations singled out by the principle of redress. This is

the principle that undeserved inequalities call for redress; and since inequalities of birth and natural endowment are undeserved, these inequalities are to be somehow compensated for.[1]

... Those who have been favored by nature, whoever they are, may gain from their good fortune only on terms that improve the situation of those who have lost out. The naturally advantaged are not to gain merely because they are more gifted, but only to cover the costs of training and education and for using their endowments in ways that help the less fortunate as well. No one deserves his greater natural capacity nor merits a more favorable starting place in society.[2]

Thus it is incorrect that individuals with greater natural endowments and the superior character that has made their development possible have a right to a cooperative scheme that enables them to obtain even further benefits in ways that do not contribute to the advantages of others. We do not deserve our place in the distribution of native endowments, any more than we deserve our initial starting place in society[3]

In his book, *Political Philosophy*[4], Steven B. Smith cites a principle that he attributes to John Rawls, taken from the latter's book, *A Theory of Justice*.

Smith contrasts Rawls' view of justice with that of John Locke (1632-1704) whose ideas inspired the founders of the United States and formed much of the basis of our Constitution.

I limit my comments on Professor Smith's book to Chapter 9. That discussion more than any other in the book drives to the heart of the individualism versus collectivism debate currently tearing our nation apart.

Smith writes on page 185 that "Rawls adds to his conception of justice something he calls the 'difference principle.' This principle maintains that our natural endowments - our talents, abilities, our family backgrounds and history, our place on the social hierarchy - are, from a moral point of view, something completely arbitrary. They are not 'ours' in any strong sense, they do not belong to us but are the result of an arbitrary genetic lottery of which each of us is the wholly undeserving beneficiary."

It is not too difficult to predict the philosophical or political drift of any society that accepts Rawls' concept of the ownership of individual endowments, and Smith does so in considerable detail. But he does not point out that Rawls' theory of justice fails to follow from Rawls' own principle. It is a non sequitur.

We have at least some plausible justification for agreeing with Rawls that our individual endowments, of whatever nature and conferred before we reach a responsible age, were gained through no effort of our own. To then claim, as Rawls did and his followers still do, that those endowment do not belong to us as individuals but to the whole of mankind, not only logically fails to follow from Rawls' statements, but refutes the whole of evolution by natural selection. If my abilities, however acquired, do not belong to me, why does it follow that they belong to everyone else? If I do not deserve my talents, why does everyone else deserve them?

Every creature that has ever existed was and is endowed with some good and some not-so-good differences from his fellows and these differences much less often than not confer some slight advantage in the struggle for survival and reproduction. That is precisely the process through which we all got here, exactly the process through which the ancestors of Professor Rawls survived to result in him and his theory.

What are justice and fairness except how humans define them? Nature's standard of justice is survival of the most adaptable, an exaction that humans overwhelmingly find repugnant and have structured their societies to try to reduce or neutralize its decree. We invent deprecations like "survival of the fittest," "law of the jungle," dog eat dog, or "Nature, red in tooth and claw" to artificially elevate ourselves above what we cannot miss seeing all around us. If we are looking for a theory of justice independent of somebody's opinion, Nature has unequivocally given us one. Most people, especially those of Rawls' persuasion, do not like that exaction from Nature, but dislike never invalidated a truth.

Any society that does not discourage individuals in their strivings and risks to fulfill their dreams will inevitably see huge disparities in wealth and accomplishment. These correspond to the huge disparities in intelligence, talent and ambition inherent in human beings. In any truly just society, the natural differences in ability and ambition will assert themselves. The most industrious, innovative and clever will rise to the top of the heap. Others will gravitate into various strata of ability and the feckless will sink to the bottom immersed in hopelessness, resentment and envy, many burning for revenge. I see *this* as justice, not the legislated equality of outcome that lies at the heart of our present politics.

Our present system offers matchless opportunities for another type of creature who focuses his sole ability and ambition on attaining authoritative office. He, and increasingly she, have demonstrated the simplicity of the formula for attaining power. Pretend to champion the common people against the monied class. Rationalize the theft (the honest word) of wealth from the accomplished and "redistribute" it to the relatively less accomplished with claims of "fairness." They enjoy applause and votes from the beneficiaries of this "generosity" and revel in the delusion of superiority, all this at little personal risk or cost.

True justice that even little children grasp before corruption from adults, implies a strong bond between effort and accomplishment. Inability, real or feigned, confers no entitlement. A great many people see this as a rank injustice and their votes, agitations, and demands that society conform to a mirage of social justice have brought to the world its most murderous despotisms.

Parental state arguments enjoy a wide emotional appeal that cannot be matched by advocates of individual responsibility. Rawls' book gained a wide following not because of the validity or lucidity of his arguments, but because he resonates so well with so many people who yearn to dump the burdens of life, and blame their own shortcomings, on those who live under more favorable circumstances. Who does not at some level in the mind want to mitigate the adversities that life throws at us and feel a bit envious of those with greater abilities or better circumstances? To this near universal yearning Rawls appeals.

No non-controversial principle of justice yet exists and most likely won't exist until we understand human nature enough to ascertain the real, that is, psychological, reasons why we adhere so fiercely to one political opinion over some other. On the way toward this receding horizon, we badly need more effective, affordable and less protracted techniques to help people overcome the effects of adverse experiences that leave enduring psychological scars. They can then elevate themselves to a level of at least some happiness and contribution to the general good.

Throughout written history people have based their definitions of justice on their religious texts and teachings of their priests. As religion has come increasingly under attack, the concept of justice has taken on an ever-increasing secular strength drawn from parental state arguments, themselves vulnerable to forceful counterarguments.

Many people see gross injustices in the huge disparities of wealth, ability and nurturing environments. Some environments are so adverse that they leave their victims psychologically scarred for life. Yet converting individual misfortunes into political problems worsens them by removing the restraint of personal responsibility. Most anguish and misfortune cannot be reversed by bureaucrats throwing yet more tax money at the problems.

We must not feel sorry for people to the extent of encouraging them to get away with their evasions of responsibility. To do so diminishes justice and advances a culture of universal dishonesty. To feel sorry for bad people while insisting that they can't help what they do betrays good people and undermines the heroic work of those few who have transcended personal adversities and brought beauty, justice, knowledge and genuine progress to our world.

This country runs on guilt. The prevailing ideology has successfully inculcated into the public mind the idea that we *owe* one another free care and feeding. The distressed, disturbed, disadvantaged, disaffected, dispossessed and myriad other dis-somethings now claim entitlement to a subsidized life. The ever-diminishing number of people who still accept an obligation to undertake meaningful work and produce something useful to earn their living have nevertheless acquiesced to the moral outrage of a counterfeit justice. They can therefore mount only the most diluted attacks against it. Good people have conceded the moral high ground to a principle that has and will continue to eviscerate all that makes a society healthy, honorable, compassionate and productive, not to mention happy. Voters want a nanny government and expect the rich to pick up the tab. *That* is the prevailing injustice in our present world.

Other than children no one is entitled to a subsidized life no matter the severity of their circumstances. In the child's temporary case the obligations fall on parents or voluntary or paid caregivers. We can and do voluntarily help those who we think deserve it. But to convert that help into a legislated moral ideal is absurd. Charity stops at the door of the legislature.

Our personalities are forged in childhood, heavily influenced by nature, nurture, culture and circumstance. Nevertheless, we still have choices. Although weighted by the noted factors, we remain fully responsible for the consequences of those choices. On the surface this looks like an injustice. How can we be held accountable for our decisions and actions over which we lack complete control? Is it not true that some people cannot help what they do?

Now consider the alternative. If I am not responsible for my thoughts and actions, who is? My every action brings consequences over the range from trivial to catastrophic. If I am allowed to escape those consequences, on whom should they fall? Dumping the consequences of my actions onto the whole of society is a rank *in*-justice. Who lacks unwelcome trials to face and limitations in facing them?

No one involuntarily owes you compensation for your misfortunes and suffering no matter how guilty or innocent you are of the causes. You must struggle with these yourself as best you can even though this offends you as an injustice.

Americans, to their peril, have lost their suspicion of government. To their deadly peril they have replaced it with whimpering mendicants and an entrenched mindset that panders to exaggerated or feigned helplessness. We show no inclination to take the painful but necessary steps to avert the political and economic catastrophe toward which we plunge.

Future historians looking back on our time should not weep too bitterly for the unprecedented tragedy that we are now preparing to unleash on ourselves and our succeeding generations. The name of this particular strain of a very old plague has been known for over a century and its purpose, methods and result for almost that long. How does one weep for victims who march knowingly into folly? One can and should weep for their innocent descendants who would not have asked to live in, or have had any part in constructing, the nightmare that they will be forced to endure or, at terrible personal risk, attempt to overthrow.

People usually make history in ignorance of the destiny they create. Yet they cannot continue to advocate a philosophy that consistently brings harm to the world and evade responsibility for that harm, no matter how their advocacy is rationalized.

After the until now unimaginable horrors bred by communism and Nazism, we must conclude that any idea can be rationalized. To what extent are the good people of the Earth responsible to prevent evil? The question should not only focus on what causes evil, but what responsibility good people must accept to prevent evil from recurring. Refocusing the question necessarily shifts responsibility for correction from the criminal to the victim, at first glance an injustice. But evil by its nature is irresponsible and therefore will rarely undertake to correct itself. The burden falls to good by default.

If we can refuse to accept the moral imperative that we *owe* free care and feeding to our fellow humans, we destroy in a stroke the prevailing myth and all its parental government derivatives and convoluted rationalizations.

To what extent must we legislate against folly or to protect reckless, feckless or helpless people from the consequences of their own mistakes? It is unreasonable and childish to expect our politicians, especially the president, to rescue us from our own poor judgment, a demand that must inevitably lead to universal dependency and its attendant despotism.

The strict evolutionist can offer a compelling argument, stripped of emotion, against the legislated compassion and accompanying statism that rule the contemporary world. This viewpoint asserts that we should allow our failures to fail, not as an act of heartless cruelty, but for self-preservation. As an analogy, bankrupt companies free resources, especially people, better applied to more efficient enterprises.

Maintaining millions of people on the public dole for entire lifetimes and sometimes across generations cannot but have a discouraging effect on those who pay the bills. The practice dampens the work incentive of the recipients and the overall efficiency of the society that practices statutory compassion.

Better that we gradually develop more effective methods to mitigate the personal tragedies and traumas that so often bring about a downward spiral of failure in those ill equipped to face adversity. In the meantime, with hypocritical compassion for the unfortunates and guilt inducements for the benefactors, our present approach encourages and perpetuates dependency in the general population and relentlessly expands authority in the government.

If Americans allow despotism to develop in this country for no better reason than a yearning for a government breast, they will have committed a heinous crime and deserve the resulting horror. Not so their kids. Bad political policy curses the generations that follow. The ones who create the dystopia are usually not the ones who have to face the consequences. With their centuries-long history of autocracy, the Russians at least have a slim excuse for tolerating continued dictatorship. With *their* incomparable heritage of freedom and unprecedented knowledge of the mistakes of history, Americans have no excuse for allowing their authoritarian government to grow like a tumor.

The world suffers from a set of related presumptions that can be summarized in a few simple statements:

I am entitled to a subsidized life.

It is the government's task to assure that all of its citizen-children are
   fed, housed, educated, doctored, found jobs, transported, compen-

sated for misfortune and mistakes, supported in retirement and finally seen off.

Since the rich accumulate their wealth by taking unfair advantage of everyone else, they must be compelled to pay a much greater share of the expenses of those less fortunate who, through no fault of their own, must struggle through life burdened with inordinate personal handicaps or circumstantial difficulties.

This looks superficially like a reasonable, fair and compassionate attitude, a consensual, liberal minded, progressive and politically correct way to think. People who hold this point of view see no bias in it. But it is instead a moral inversion that already rushes headlong toward social, economic and political catastrophe. In pursuit of an illusion of social justice we rush headlong on a road to hell.

Prevailing political commentary has given us plausible arguments that appeal to our innate compassion and sense of fairness. They contemptuously dismiss opposing arguments as reactionary, obstructive and outmoded. But all of the alleged benefits imply unrestrained expansion of government. A wise reading of history shows us that permitting governments to grow into big ugly tumors has not resulted in healthy freedom-respecting societies.

What is just about indolence or prodigality riding subsidized or free on the back of self-motivation and thrift? What is just about someone riding on the back of a person who does not want him there? The idea creates a deadly collusion between those who demand a free ride and those who promise to give it to them in exchange for authoritative office and delusions of moral superiority.

The rage and acrimony that so characterize our present political conflict is not that difficult to understand. If you knew someone who wanted to harm those you love, your anger would be understandable and justified, would it not? Apply that question to the nation you love. The concept applies to any faction in the present debate.

The universal yearning to mitigate the brutality and brevity of life is the fundamental force animating all political doctrines and movements.

If statists finally achieve the society that they have tried so hard for so long to bring into being, it will not resemble the notion of social justice that they had in mind. Then unable to admit that their ideas were the chief cause of their nation's decline, they will begin the search for "enemies of the people" who "betrayed the revolution." We have seen this morbid drama acted out so many times in so many places that it has become a lurid tragedy written, produced and staged by mountebanks. Name a better example of willful corruption of societal health. We are not dealing here with ignorance or good intentions.

If the dream of an easier life at other people's expense is ever to be surrendered, we must come to understand why its fulfillment forever eludes us and stop blaming that other political party, that other religion or that opposing ideology for blocking the dream.

The dream is intrinsically, inherently, inhumanly *unjust* because it dumps the costs and responsibilities of maintaining the easy rider's life onto others who neither want nor deserve that burden. Because it fosters dependency, irresponsibility, demagoguery, deceitful politicians, bloated government, acclaims mediocrity over skill development and admirable accomplishment, depreciates the currency, vilifies the most productive people in the society, demoralizes the citizenry and bankrupts the economy. This debilitating sequence will invariably sink a community of a few or a nation of tens or hundreds of millions. What creature has ever appeared on this planet that was able to escape the struggle for survival save the one complicitly seduced by self-delusions, the only one capable of dishonesty?

"In order to justify itself the socialist plan conscripts every institution and even language to its purpose. For example, it describes the enforced economic equality at which it aims as 'social justice', even though it can be achieved only by the unjust expropriation of assets gained by free agreements. The true meaning of justice, [F. A.]

Hayek argues, is that given by Aristotle and followed by Ulpian in the digest of the Roman law — the practice giving to each person what is due. But the word 'social' sucks the meaning out of 'justice'. Social justice is not a form of justice at all, but a form of moral corruption. It means rewarding people for feckless behavior, for neglecting their own and their family's wellbeing, for breaking their agreements and for exploiting their employers."[5]

We have already reached the point where this concept has passed beyond the moral and philosophical and entered the compass of simple arithmetic. We cannot afford the society that so many people erroneously describe as just. The money simply is not there. Observe Southern Europe. What's the end point? Financial and moral bankruptcy? Most Americans don't know it, but we are already there. Bankruptcy is what happens when voters demand benefits that their grandchildren cannot pay for and elect demagogues on promises that have no hope of fulfillment. When people demand something for nothing, they get nothing for something. Today this is called justice, a travesty with few parallels.

I would love to be able to inculcate autonomy and responsibility into every individual mind such that demagoguery and tyranny become impossible and freedom need not be periodically repurchased with the blood of courage.

A letter to Parental Government Voters: You complain that you cannot find housing within your means, or a job that pays what you think you are worth, or inexpensive food for your table, or afford a good school for your kids, or think yourself a victim of the rich, or abused and offended by hateful bigots, or feel ostracized because of your uncommon sexual orientation, or suffered a nasty childhood, or watched your dreams shatter, or the society of which you are part fails to conform to your fantasy of social justice? I am sorry. These are truly regrettable circumstances. Life is tough for everybody, even those for whom it seems otherwise.

But now I must add one more to your collection of perceived injustices. To discourage dependency, irresponsibility and the demagoguery that feeds on those two, a thriving society must deny you entitlement to involuntary compensation for your real or affected misfortunes and inadequacies. You will have to struggle a bit to survive just like every animal, insect and plant in the world whatever its endowment or circumstances. Our countless ancestors had, in profound ignorance, to overcome countless adversities to result in you and me. What a damned inconvenience that you should not be able to lean on those more able or fortunate. Outrageous, isn't it? What fiend would impose such a heartless decree?

She is called Nature.

NOTES

1 John Rawls, *A Theory of Justice*, Revised Edition, The Belkamp Press of Harvard University Press, Cambridge, MA, 1971, 1999, p86.
2 Rawls, p87.
3 Rawls, p89.
4 Yale University Press, New Haven and London, 2012.
5 Roger Scruton, *Conservatism*, All Points Books, 2017, p110. Punctuation follows British convention.

POWER FROM CHAOS

THE QUESTION HAS PUZZLED ME FOR YEARS and other thinkers far longer, how do power mad people achieve mastery over huge populations?

Identifying examples does not tax the imagination. Lenin, Hitler, Stalin, Mao and the somewhat less murderous psychopaths in that clan have soaked history in blood, tears and tragedy. Lenin once remarked that power was lying in the streets and he and his sycophants only needed to pick it up. Circumstances in his time and place made his grab possible. It would not have worked in another place and time. Why these particular circumstances? War? Political upheaval? Loss of respect for or confidence in political authority? Crumbling moral certainties being gradually replaced by others less secure? A critical mass of people demanding something they cannot have and mesmerized by demagogues who promise to deliver it? All these speculations merit consideration but fail to explain why evil always triumphs out of moral chaos. Following the disintegration of a polity, why must despotism always emerge from the rubble?

The 20th Century suffered the rise to power the most brutal despots in history: Lenin, Stalin, Hitler, Mao, Pol Pot, Kim Jung Sung and his descendants, and the lesser pretenders to political wisdom like Mussolini, Franco, Khadafi, Assad, Castro, Chavez and those still nursing their delusions of grandeur in the former Soviet "republics." Tyrants in past centuries seemed less brutal only for lack of the means and a large and vulnerable enough population, not for lack of will.

Why does this continue?

The continuing disintegration of religious authority probably contributed, but its restoration has no hope of correcting the authoritarian pathology that plagues us.

Each of the named individuals seized power at a time of political chaos, economic collapse and much noise from myriad social theorists with conflicting remedies for social salvation that they propose to force onto an entire population.

Many times has history recorded the overthrow of some political order only to see it replaced with one much worse. That happened numerous times in the 20th Century alone in Russia, Germany, Italy, China, Korea, and several African, South American and other Asian countries.

The specter now looms over the United States. All we need is a political upheaval like a major war or massive inflation, the latter on our horizon. Shall the government keep churning out dollars until their value is not worth the cost of printing them? Then what? Do you really want to know how that drama plays out? It has been staged many times. Look at Germany's 1920s inflation and what sort of creature "rescued" Germans from their self-imposed folly with a catastrophe. You think that this cannot happen here? Guess again.

I once pictured the successful development of autocracy as a coin, the leader on the head and everybody else on the tail. I now think that a triad or an upright equilateral triangle serves as a better metaphor. The leader sits atop the peak like a demigod and passes down his imperious whims. His enforcers, holding a second vertex at the bottom, carry out his wishes with various blends of obedient enthusiasm and brutality.

The third, and now powerless bottom vertex, suffers the consequences of their prior refusal to grasp the nature of whom they supported. They were more or less willing dupes who, with varying degrees of complicity, empowered the despot and made the malignant structure possible.

Much different motivations animate each point of the triangle. What drives the despot is ironically the simplest to analyze. He (usually a he) typically seethes with rage, hatred, malice, and vengeance, each of those misdirected, their true sources unacknowledged and unexamined. Not a trace of insight disturbs his deranged view of reality. Lenin, Stalin, Hitler and maybe Mao (I've not studied him) left us useful paradigms. Each suffered a perverse childhood that engendered the rage and malice that permanently warped and scarred his personality and permitted him to inflict his murderous hatred on all within his power. A fusion of rage, hatred and political power creates the world's most lethal force. It has infected many of history's dictators who have brought so much death and devastation to humanity. The greater the eagerness to rule, the less the fitness to rule.

To understand what drives any adult personality we must thoroughly examine that individual's childhood experiences. Although such an exploration daunts us with great difficulty, especially in the cases of the people mentioned here, the answers that we seek and desperately need will be found nowhere else. To finally put a stop to the all too frequent rise of such people who have infected the world with their contagion, we must come to understand what circumstances bring about their peculiar and destructive pathology and neutralize those circumstances to the extent possible without cruelty.

The second prong of the triad presents us with a more difficult puzzle. Hitler's well-studied twelve-year regime left us with the best historical example of a phenomenon that on our peril we must come to thoroughly understand as a psychopathology that did not end with Nazi Germany. Hitler's Third Reich was not unique, only better documented than the even more hideous despotisms of Stalin and Mao. Hitler's instruments of enforcement, chiefly the SS and the Gestapo, were infested with human robots selected and programmed to such a degree of unquestioning obedience as to be able to dispassionately commit genocidal murder. But these men (and very few women) were not machines. They were human. They had brains. They had the capacity to consider what they were doing. Why then did they submit to such abject obeisance like zombies? That question in itself would make a worthy study in psychopathology beyond my capabilities.

Then what about the sick people who commanded the zombies? Wasn't their guilt much greater, people like Himmler, Goebbels, Heydrich, Göring and the "angel of death" physician, Josef Mengele? What inner demons drove *them*?

We come to the third corner of this depraved triangle. Millions of people, hysterical and teary eyed, wildly cheered the triumph of their savior. Savior from what remains an open question. We have seen this drama played out in the 20th Century with starring roles for Hitler, Mussolini, Castro, Chavez and a few less notorious but equally duplicitous protagonists. Were these cheerleaders stupid? Did they not see what their hero would shortly bring them? Fail to see his deceit? Or were they complicit in a gigantic fraud much like accessories in a crime? What did these masses really want? Certainly not what they claimed such as social or any other kind of justice. What then? Revenge against alleged exploiters? Punitive action against some hated group set up as scapegoats to blame for and deny complicity in the destruction of their own society? Dumping life's responsibilities and burdens onto those allegedly better off? Or are we dealing with causes much deeper than those superficial speculations, evocations of passions rooted in the familial nurturing of long ago, now forgotten but still powerfully pulling puppet strings unseen and unacknowledged from above the stage?

I must also mention the apologists and thousands of thinkers, journalists, professors, commentators, writers, cinematographers and countless dupes still with us all over the world who lend the authority of their offices or influence over their readers and listeners to rationalize the developing nightmare. These are the worst of all the participants because they have the intelligence, education and, just as importantly, freedom, to know and act better. They are even more guilty than the despot they empower, people like the philosopher Martin Heidegger who rationalized Hitler's regime and the countless apologists outside Germany and Russia who wrote panegyrics praising Lenin's murderous usurpation of power and rationalizations for Stalin's manic brutality.

Two questions crying out for answers receive not so much as a nod of acknowledgement in all the rancor that poisons contemporary debates:

1. What familial and cultural circumstances result in haters like Marx and murderers like Mao, Stalin, Hitler and Pol Pot who have used Marx to rationalize their tyranny?

2. Why do so many people eagerly allow themselves to be seduced by these charlatans until it is too late to re-chain the escaped genocidal maniac at which time they cry that this is not what they had in mind?

Both questions are psychological and strongly suggest that the population seduced by the duplicity of the charlatans are not innocent of complicity. What do voters *really* want and expect?

German voters were not innocent victims of Hitler's murderous ideas and policies. Venezuelans *elected* Hugo Chavez who immediately set in motion that country's precipitous decline from wealth to national penury. American voters cannot escape responsibility for the lies and moral inversions that presently engulf them and seriously threaten to destroy the incomparable nation that their founding fathers gave them.

Voters rationalize their complicity in theft-by-proxy by falsely claiming victimization by alleged exploiters that supposedly entitles them to unearned compensation. Who is the more guilty here? The dishonest voters or the rulers who regard their duped victims as contemptible pawns in the expansion of power?

Voters cannot get away with the excuse that the budding tyrants hid their intentions during their rise. Their duplicity is never so obscure as to evade detection. Hitler wrote a book clearly outlining what he was going to do. Ditto Lenin. Saul Alinsky wrote an instruction manual to guide neophyte statists. [1]

Unmistakable hatred pours out of these writings like the blood and tears that will pour out of the coming victims. Voters cannot escape accusations of complicity when they elect a liar who promises to deliver unearned benefits by stealing from the rich.

The evil now spreads its tendrils into the United States. Those who, appalled, watch helplessly the malignancy metastasize into every healthy organ of the political body and have at least some rational assessment of the causes, are too few in number to have much to say in the matter. The voices who now cry in the wilderness will later find themselves caged in a nightmare. They can then speak out only at great peril to themselves. Such heroic people try to be heard and read, their voices floundering in the prevailing deluge of inanity.

I fear the stage is being set for a replay of 1920-1945 Germany. Our present debt crisis and the hyperinflation to surely follow will release the bomb that destroys the tattered remnants of what the founding fathers gave us. Voters will then cry for a political messiah to save them from the consequences of their own folly. He will dutifully rise like a specter from a swamp of deceit and murder the bleeding spirit of honor.

We have not awakened from the nightmare. The absurd "woke" culture that infects our information media is but a small piece of the nightmare from which we must awaken to save our nation from the malignancy killing it.

The journalism profession has sold its soul to an ignoble cause. Its members have become pimps for statism. With so much that its practitioners could constructively contribute to the betterment of mankind, they have instead overwhelmingly chosen to ride the leftist train to catastrophe. They see no bias in their world view, at least not a harmful one. Moral righteousness has displaced the self-reflection essential to any honest assessment of reality. We all are victims of their blind arrogance.

As bad as this situation has been described, journalism, especially its news commentating component, is not the principal inciter of our present sociopolitical furor. I give that dubious honor to American education K through PhD whose practitioners are forcing the rest of us to reap what they have sown. Please read the related essay.

When reading conservative literature such as *National Review, Washington Examiner* or the *Wall Street Journal*, I often detect a religious undercurrent. I also can't help noticing what is not there: the overarching question *why*. The troubles and conflicts of the world are presented in lurid detail and blame assigned to that other hopelessly deluded political party. What we do not read is any exploration about why the listed and earlier horrors of history perennially recur and what might constitute the fundamental cause.

I want to cry out to these writers that adoption of their viewpoint, their religion, is not going to save us. Religion as a foundation for morals or intelligent discourse is dying. These writers cannot save it and should not try. Principles derived from religion rest on quicksand.

When I read "liberal" literature such as the *New York Times* or *Time* magazine, a similar argument comes to mind. I want to cry out to these writers that your statist doctrine has brought unparalleled woe to the historical record. It cannot save us and your promotion of it skirts the edge of the criminal.

A proclamation we often read or hear about:

It's not my fault that I'm poor. It's not my fault that rich people live in their fine houses and I don't have enough to eat. They steal from the poor. That's our money. There should be no rich and poor, but everyone equal. I have rights to free medical care, decent housing, free education and enough to eat. We blame the greedy capitalists for all the misery in this country. Without them all would be fair and happy. The system that fails to provide these basic needs is wrong and should be overthrown. People who like this system extract obscene profits from it. They are exploiters, thieves, reactionaries and backward thinking. Our way is liberal, progressive, compassionate and fair minded.

Demagogues and future tyrants listen to all this with keen interest, salivate and plot.

I have raised many questions but posed few answers because I do not know them. I suspect that when and if such answers finally come to us, they will have gradually emerged from increasing *individual* self-awareness and understanding. I emphasize *individual* to head off the inevitable refocus on collective causes and remedies, the welfare state ethos, the all-pervasive evasion and transfer of responsibility that sickens mankind, the sickness that assigns every problem to *we* instead of to *me*.

That we do not know ourselves at all well, why we believe and behave as we do, is *the* fundamental enduring human curse.

To understand the motivation of those who crave to rule, we must dig down below what appears on the surface. Such people obviously want power. But why? Contentment cannot be found in power because it is never sufficient to satisfy a passion for revenge for an unidentifiable injustice long since passed beyond any hope of redress.

If it were possible to dig through the layers of lies, duplicity, envy, hubris, hypocritical promises, rationalized violence, cynical debasement of scrupulous comportment and contempt for responsibility, we would eventually reach the cellar of resentments that fumes deep inside every depraved personality. Therein we would gaze upon a hurt, crying, lonely, angry child wanting to strike back at whatever he imagines to be the source of his torment. His hatred and rage burn unanchored to their real cause and are therefore free to pour out upon the uncomprehending world.

Wrath of a Nihilist

I will rub your noses in my pathology before I dispossess, then murder you. Once a nobody, I am now a *somebody* who you shall not ignore but learn to obey, fear and burn into your daily thoughts. I will bow your head and bend your knee.

Since I cannot create meaning, I will create destruction and call it deconstruction. What you admire I will vulgarize. What you love I will hate. What you value I will trash. Whom you venerate I will desecrate. What you honor I will corrupt. What you treasure I will steal. What you build I will pull down. What you think true I will obscure into confusion. What brings you happiness I will drown in tears. I scorn your virtues and pretentious pursuit of truth. Think you beyond the reach of terror? Watch me and I will savagely teach you your error. Those "useful idiots"[2] who applaud my rise will be the first to taste my rage. I will exploit every crisis real or invented to further that rise.

I am the born-again sophist, the relativist, the envier and hater of your absurd presumption of freedom. I am the consequence of your evasion of reality and your intransigent insistence that your theistic or political religion must cherry pick evidence and override facts. I am the totalitarian whom you are nurturing and will return the favor with sneering contempt. I am the harbinger of pain and grief. I am malice. I am chaos. I am death.

You think the Four Horsemen of the Apocalypse a myth?[3] I am all four and mock your naivety while I add two more to the four, terror and tyranny. You will feel my enmity on your back. I am the perversion of reality. I will confuse then crush you under lies, deceit, duplicity and sorrow, impose every manner of ideological absurdity, invert the meaning of every word essential for an understanding of what I will do to you while I jeer your credulity.

"Evil be thou my Good."[4]

NOTES

1   *Rules for Radicals*, 1989.
2   Lenin's contemptuous sarcasm directed against Western "liberals."
3   Death, Famine, War, and Conquest.
4   John Milton put these words into the mouth of Satan in *Paradise Lost*, Book Four.

REFLECTIONS ON AMERICAN EDUCATION

F EW SUBJECTS IN CONTEMPORARY AMERICAN DEBATES elicit as much pro and con passion as education. A brief essay that pretends to address a subject that would fill a library must compromise, then grudgingly accept the resultant distortions. One of these is picturing American Education as a monolithic entity, a conflation partially justified by a few principles that have become ascendant in K through PhD schools.

Academia's zealots can hardly credit their institution for improving social health. Their problems are too manifest. The philosophical errors of the education community cannot be criticized without an implicit indictment of the culture with which it is fused and from which it receives enormous support. Nevertheless, the current debate is vital to clarify the purpose of education and address whether educational institutions are fulfilling that purpose at a cost commensurate with the benefits they offer.

The familiar bumper sticker, "If you think education is expensive, try ignorance," ignorantly misses the point of the present controversy. No one with an IQ above 73 argues in favor of ignorance. The bumper sticker jabs at an obvious straw man and therefore raises the suspicion that the diversion is deliberate. Away from what does it wish to deflect our attention?

Debates boil or freeze with either hot advocacy or brain-dead entrenchment of some ideology. What are schools explicitly and implicitly teaching?

Do these teachings help or cripple? Do they attempt to illuminate objective reality or subtly confine discussion within the political and sociological ideology of an entrenched system of related ideas? More succinctly, are schools centers of vital knowledge and free inquiry or cloisters dedicated to indoctrination?

We must begin to answer these questions somewhere and the motto of a Denver, Colorado area school district is as good a place as any: "To provide a quality education that prepares all children for a successful future."

The statement is bland enough to avoid controversy by accommodating virtually all definitions of "quality education" or "successful future," and that was probably one of the principal motivations of its adoption because those definitions are wrenched about at the center of the very debate being evaded. Like the bumper sticker, the motto attempts to say something meaningful but uncontroversial and fails both. I for one would prefer to see much greater emphasis on respecting reason, learning to think critically, exposing errors of logic, and rigorously and therefore controversially defining "quality education" and "successful future."

Readily available statistics that focus on the levels of learning among American students in comparisons with those from other countries, and the related costs per student, make pretty sobering and disturbing reading. Defenders of American education attempt to explain away these widely publicized figures as "distortions of the true picture," an often read excuse that leaves us wondering what their "true" picture looks like. They can blame the family, the wider culture, that eternal complaint -- lack of money, or anything else they like, but they simply cannot escape those glaring and damning numbers. In any case, arguments are predicated on the questionable assumption that enlightenment is the primary objective.

Other Americans in increasing numbers are reaching the conclusion that they are not getting what they pay for, our educational institutions are irredeemably corrupt. The corruption is philosophical in nature and maddeningly difficult to pin down in the fog of excuses, diversions, distortions, evasions and half truths spewed out by the teaching profession's ideological

REFLECTIONS ON AMERICAN EDUCATION | 113

hegemony. Whoever you choose to believe in this confusing debate, a great many if not a majority of people agree that something is profoundly wrong. Even the system's administrators now offer concessions in the form of empty slogans like "performance promises" that mollify without touching the ideological undercurrent that riles so many people who remain convinced they are victims of a swindle.

Exactly what is that ideological undercurrent that incenses religious fundamentalists who sniff impiety everywhere, flares the ready suspicions of leftists paranoid about corporate greed, rankles apostles of the market economy who point to the creeping socialist demon, alarms humanists who express no fear of expanding State control, yet manage to find a fundamentalist roaming every academic corridor, and worries the beleaguered thinker who would love to see respect for objective reason and critical thinking dethrone gushing touchy-feely emotionalism, political indoctrination, cries for "social justice" and cultural diversity?

As with all of us, long forgotten unconscious impressions etched during our early years strongly influence attitudes and choices that much later show up on the behavioral surface. Speculations about what unconscious convictions might be motivating teachers' choices for classroom instruction are explored later in this essay.

Among the surface principles that influence the choices of vocal teaching and instructional materials, I touch on only a few, all errors, that dominate education administrations, and can at least be mentioned with fairness in this brief essay. All have considerable overlapping interdependency and enjoy ascendancy in the wider society.

Everything is relative. Certainty is an illusion. Death and taxes are the only absolutes. Truth is an illusion. I go with my feelings. I feel that _____ is true (fill in the blank with your most impassioned belief). The only reality is internal. All we can know for certain is that we know nothing.

Please note that every one of these statements contradicts itself, yet they form the foundation of a prevalent cultural trend, well entrenched in and emanating from academia, that eschews and even scorns the extremely difficult search for truth. The entire bloody and tearful history of thought has been a heroic struggle of the pitiful few against the uncountable minions who sense reality with the warmth of their guts, for whom thinking is not a process of weighing evidence and inducing or deducing conclusions which must then be tested, but consists of recitations from a tiny breviary of stereotyped responses stretched to cover any arising contingency. For such people feelings preside over reason.

Although frequently cited, religious bigotry is not the sole culprit. The ceaseless war between faith and reason rages far beyond the borders of theistic religion. Secular religions defend their sacred texts with equal ferocity. For examples we need look no further than Marxism and more recently the insidious concept of political correctness that spread like a cancer from the dogmatic arrogance of secular academia.

The education-at-any-cost mentality of those in K through PhD institutions value their teaching fads and obfuscations above other considerations. As the sole solution to their institutional problems, they perennially cry for more money to fund their ever fluid notions, always promoted with a pious concern for children and college kids. You could throw gold bricks at these people and they would suck them up like butter blocks fed to a blast furnace, and our young people would still not receive a better education in the bargain. Fiscal responsibility acquires a strange definition in the supposedly erudite halls of academia.

Often heard in K-12 circles is the grand-sounding proclamation that all children must receive a good education. All? No matter the cost? From curious to somnambulant? From eager to obstinate? From cooperative to disruptive? From genius to dolt? At what intellectual cost to the bright students and fiscal cost to the financiers if that education is diluted to the dolt's level? And what does "good" mean? Good for whom? For what? And the salient question today: what is the political, social, economic or religious agenda of those lessons? "No child left behind" is a bromide prescribed as a remedy.

Do we really want to put ourselves, children and grandchildren in hock to humanity's lowest common denominator?

The concept of cultural diversity has become one of those hot fads that emerge like ephemeral sparks out of the smoke of educators. The idea of course is to inculcate a tolerance for all cultures with never any invitation to judge the good from the not so good. In practice the idea has resulted in praises for every culture on Earth except our own. Can anyone actually make the absurd claim that the Athens of Pericles rose no higher than the Kabul of the Taliban? Or that the variegated pulsing vitality of New York City is not superior to contemporary Saudi Arabia still arrested in a 7th Century straight jacket?

I abhor rap "music" and the aggressive and vulgar males who insist that everyone must share their culture blasted across a city park or out their open car window. Why must I?

I would not care to live in Kandahar, Nanking or Koudougou (West Africa) and I am not criticizing the climate. I prefer a culture that values the freedom to think. I prefer to derive truth from thought and empirical observation instead of by consulting some unquestioned doctrine, feeling visceral warmth, calculating planetary influences on personality or seeking divine guidance. Why must I value these fatuous approaches to truth, prevalent in virtually all cultures including our own?

I do not value theocratic cultures like Iran, oligarchies like China, autocracies like North Korea or the defunct Soviet Union that lay a heavy hand of authority over the mind. They cannot hold a candle to the admittedly flawed culture of the United States. Schools have much better ideas to emphasize than cultural diversity, like maybe how to think critically about the bilge pouring out of academia.

Americans cannot expect to preserve a society that leads the world in discovery unless its educational system fosters the tough objective thinking that nurtures and protects a free and idea-advancing nation. Nor can we expect bright immigrants to continue to furnish a significant fraction of our scientific leadership. Nor does any other than an illusory battle rage between science and something else. There is no something else. Science with its flaws remains the only way we have to understand our universe and within it the blue speck we call home.

Reformers will look with futility to the educational system's leadership for meaningful solutions. The fox is not about to provide sound advice about chicken wire.

An even more insidious teaching doctrine recently erupted in a controversy in the State of Virginia when parents discovered that their children were being taught Critical Race Theory as part of their K-12 teaching. Former governor and later unsuccessful candidate for the same office, Terry McAuliffe, ignited further outrage when he declared on September 28, 2021 — a remark for which he later apologized — that, "I don't think parents should be telling schools what they should teach."

One might well wonder to whom McAuliffe apologized. To the angry parents whose children were being subjected to political indoctrination sneaked into their lessons? Or to his like-minded partisans for letting the cat out of the bag, disclosing their covert agenda?

McAuliffe's defenders hastened to quench the flames by claiming that his comment was taken out of context. We would be challenged to find a valid justification for such a statement in *any* context.

In a September 29, 2021 letter to President Biden, the National School Boards Association denied that Critical Race Theory was being taught in K-12 public schools and asked Mr. Biden for help from law enforcement officials to monitor "the threat levels" … "to public schoolchildren, educators, board members, and facilities/campuses. We also request the assistance of the U.S. Postal Inspection Service to intervene against threatening letters and cyberbullying attacks that have been transmitted to students, school board members, district administrators, and other educators."[1]

Are these alleged threats real, exaggerated protests from irate parents, deliberate diversions from acknowledging the cause of parents' outrage, or a revealing example of the neurotic deflection trick of acting like the abused and wounded instead of the offender?

Are parents mistaken in their accusations of political indoctrination of their children? The current nationwide protests from parents could scarcely derive from an illusion. Parents are seeing the results in the horror stories their kids bring home from school. One such horror story popped into the news on October 31, 2021, appropriately on Halloween:

> A Loudoun County, Virginia, mom said at a school board meeting this month that she pulled her children from the public school system after her 6-year-old asked her if she was «born evil» because she's white.

> "We had specifically moved them out of LCPS [Loudoun County Public Schools] due to the swift and uncompromising political agenda of Superintendents Williams, Ziegler, and the school board had forced upon us. First, it was in the early spring of 2020 when my six-year-old somberly came to me and asked me if she was born evil because she was a white person. Something she learned in a history lesson at school," the mother said at a school board meeting on Oct. 26. Video of her testimony has since spread on social media.[2]

Sneaky political indoctrination, blatant or covert, is a subterfuge hardly limited to Virginia. Critical Race Theory is only one of the numerous leftist pasture droppings fouling American Schools K through PhD. The chicanery is particularly onerous when imposed on vulnerable elementary school kids, conditioning their innocent minds for much worse to follow.

I oppose *religion* in all of its manifestations. The word is placed in italics because I expand its common theistic understanding to include any *belief*, that is, any faith, ideology, dogma, doctrine and the like that so enthralls individuals that in their minds the beliefs trump all evidence and all arguments to the contrary no matter how compelling. The *belief*, neither science nor evidence, forms the rock-hard foundation of their views of reality, morality, concepts of right and wrong and guides them thru life.

To them the belief is the unquestioned axiomatic truth. It is exactly that lack of respect for the pursuit of truth and the unyielding unquestioning hold on belief that precludes self-understanding and thereby becomes the fount of human-created misery, mutual distrust, hatred and war. It is also why I do not like the word *believe* or any of its relatives. It is the blind acceptance of something as true without further consideration. Given that definition, beliefs can be applied to anything, specific to this discussion the theistic and the political *religions* being taught in our educational system. Truth to a theist is whatever he finds in his "holy" book. Truth to a leftist is whatever promotes his political agenda, both unmistakably religions.

If we want to see the primary source of the malignancy currently metastasizing into every vital organ of the political body, we must look left toward K through PhD education. The junk being taught in classrooms throughout the land is pure poison to immature minds indoctrinated before they have sufficient understanding and power of critical thinking to effectively challenge the babble being dumped into their heads.

I experienced a bit of this myself during my mercifully brief enrollment in a philosophy class at the University of Colorado[3] graduate school. We "studied," if that's the right word, the French obscurantist philosopher, Jacques Derrida (1930-2004)[4] who spoke and wrote in such gibberish that "even the French gave up on him," according to another professor at CU. The comment begged for an answer to the question, why was this man's opaque writing assigned reading at the University of Colorado? Since no one could decipher what Derrida meant, the CU professor could decrypt him anyway she wanted with little concern that she might have to provide clarification to a puzzled student.

How Derrida managed to win a place at the head of a classroom (in France) was a criminal injustice against students struggling to comprehend reality and being fed drivel. He was one of the innumerable sources of the cognitive cancer that long ago floated across the Atlantic as a corrosive fog where the like-minded breathed it in and who, like now, needed to bury their true intentions in obscure language. The cancer began to spread into the vitals of our universities where it continues to eat away whatever is sensible and healthy.

Deconstruction defined: diminish the great, the good, the beautiful, the venerated, the heroic, the skilled and the admirably accomplished down to the level of the confused, the trite, the ineffectual and the meaningless, down to the level of the deconstructionist. Defame the noble and commemorate trash. Build a heroic edifice, then observe the deconstructionists, incapable of imagining anything uplifting and envious of those capable of building anything, begin to tear it down.

If we look through history at the thinkers who have brought real progress to our conflicted world, always opposed by the ruling doctrinaires, we do not see them teaching absurdities like cultural diversity, deconstruction, post modernism, post structuralism, or the scribblings of obscurantist philosophers; nor did they cloak themselves with pretentious flatteries like liberal, progressive, egalitarian, socially just, avant-garde, fair minded, well meaning, compassionate and presumptions of a "deeper" understanding.

Derrida and those like him are close, but not the worst source of the problem. Derrida was just an obfuscating con man. The world has no shortage of such people but we commit a criminal act against young minds when we place them at the heads of classrooms.

How do people like him gain such influence? What administrators decided that these people should be awarded tenure to indoctrinate young minds? What politicos decided that such people deserve subsidized salaries? Here is where we see the faces of our destruction, those unseen pullers of strings above the stage covertly spreading their disease.

K-12 teachers and college professors represent a *somewhat* less onerous threat than the unions who claim to represent them and the administrators who hire them, impose teaching standards and advance the malignancy unseen from outside the classroom.

If students and/or parents had to directly pay out-of-pocket for a university curriculum to prepare for an unsubsidized, remunerative and meaningful career in some private risk-assuming endeavor, be assured that none of the following would be among the subjects chosen: critical race theory, woke ideology, cancel culture, q-anon, intersectionality, identity politics, standpoint theory, micro-aggression theory, structuralism, post-structuralism, deconstruction, political "science" (What is scientific about politics?), urban studies, gender and sexuality studies, feminist studies, population studies, transnational feminist theory, ethnography, queer theory, the oxymoron postmodernism, social justice, or the worst of the lot, Marxism.

I am not making these up. None will be difficult to find in major university catalogs or course descriptions.

We come to the salient question, the all-important *why*?

If we persist in assigning the wrong causes to harmful political trends, solutions will forever elude us. Obscurantist gibberish pouring out of university humanities departments evokes the suspicion of some clandestine intent. The professors' pretentious claims to a better understanding of human nature and their cries for what they call social justice disguise something neither true, just nor admitted. We are dealing with an unhealthy and hidden purpose. Based on what they preach and what they profess to hate, these people unmistakably campaign for a totalitarian world order. Since such political structures have already demonstrated themselves as history's signal catastrophes, thinking minds can scarcely avoid asking the question *why*. And now we must enter the fog-enshrouded realm of the unconscious.

Would any rational person hire any of the following?

- A pathological liar to teach moral principles
- An inveterate hater to teach the meaning of justice
- A geography instructor who believes in a flat earth
- An astronomy professor who teaches an earth-centered universe
- A pool lifeguard who can't swim

Then why are there Marxists in our universities indoctrinating minds with the deadliest and most disastrously failed dogma in history? Who places such deceivers at the heads of university classrooms where they can spread their pathogen into the immature young minds they are betraying? And why are they able to achieve such national notoriety almost overnight?

In academia can be found much of the source of the socialist-loving America-hating malignancy eating the vital organs of this great country. It is there we must direct our assault.

What really drives these professors, the administrators who hire them and the media that spread their contagion? If not to inculcate their individual students with autonomous inquiry, critical thinking, responsibility and enlightenment, a deficiency manifestly evident, what then? Certainly nothing so noble as the pursuit of truth or that current facade, social justice.

Since they are causing so much harm, the time has come to at least make some attempt to expose the psychological undercurrents that carry these people along. We cannot peer inside these people's heads and see what operates therein, but the survival of our sanity, and likely much else, demands that at least we give it an honest try.

I cannot know what deep down drives these people but offer a few speculations:

- A statist government with their kind in charge?
- A subterfuge to mask envy and/or hatred?
- Evasion of an admission of irrelevance?
- Timidity?
- Reluctance to admit an aversion to risk?
- Lack of imagination or ambition?
- A groundless presumption that their vital profession entitles them to tenure laws and subsidized salaries?
- A delusion of "higher" understanding of the human condition?

- Avoidance of embarrassment in comparison to more accomplished people such as financially successful entrepreneurs or the spectacular discoveries of scientists?

We can gain a hint toward an answer from their vocal hatred of capitalists and the rich in general that often look so vindictive and punitive that it immediately prompts the questions, for what are these people being vilified? Because the hated ones succeeded and exposed the lesser ambitions or greater risk-aversion of the haters who rationalize their envy and malice with false accusations of exploitation and injustice while entertaining their delusions of moral superiority?

Does envy of the financial success of businessmen and the spectacular success of scientists in discovering the guarded secrets of Nature account for the intellectual's —especially non science academics' — hatred of capitalism and adherence to collectivist ideology? How else do we explain prestige-stealing pretenses like political "science" and similar self flatteries? They delude themselves with, "We too are scientists." What can possibly be scientific about politics in which, contrary to real science, conclusions are preordained, then rationalized? Teachers of this parody complete the theft with a ludicrous presumption of superior sensitivity to the human condition.

Obscurantists delude themselves into imagining that they have discovered some profound truth beyond the grasp of ordinary mortals and assure that their readers and listeners never catch on that these poseurs haven't the foggiest idea what they are talking about. The travesty amounts to a gigantic fraud of both perpetrators and dupes.

As a plausible alternative, we can suppose that the haters don't care to spend their lives pursuing profit, but see other paths as more noble, meaningful and personally fulfilling. Fine for them, but that fails to explain the hate and those choices confer no entitlement to remuneration from presumed low-life money grubbers, nor do they relieve the obligation to live honorably and earn one's way through life.

It would seem that lefty professors are reaping what they have sown: success for them in betraying young minds and paving the road to authoritative government, but tragedy for humanity. Dr. Frankenstein cannot escape responsibility for the monster he created by protesting that the evil result of his labors was not what he had in mind. But evil was and is in the minds of the rabid nihilists of the 1960s and their ideological progeny now in control of our K through PhD schools.

Any avowal of Marxism, the most murderous and catastrophic doctrine in history, exposes the hypocrisy of humanities professors, leaders of Black Lives Matter, political commentators and our culture haters who deceitfully proclaim their devotion to justice.

Many factors contribute to the decline of the United States. But if I had to narrow the list of contributors to a principle one, it would be the American education system. The college kids who scream *fascist* and *racist* at people undeserving of those insults, and who love to raise hell on campuses and streets, insult the police and demand a free life are being taught incivility by their lefty professors. Their contumacious behavior is a consequence, perhaps unintended but more likely not, of being taught that all is culturally relative, truth is a social construct, all opinions are of equal value, no culture is better than another but only different, all ethnic groups are equal, anyone's opinion is as valid as any other, who's to say what is right, and worst of all, capitalism is unfairly exploitative, must be destroyed and socialism offers the only hope for a socially just egalitarian world.

An unacknowledged emotional undercurrent set in motion inside every child profoundly influences all later adult thinking. This accounts for much of the political animosity convulsing the contemporary world. We are tied for life to what happened long ago, what did not happen, what should have happened but did not, and what did happen but should not have.

I do not suppose that the college kids screaming fascist at people they don't like are really angry at what they claim to be angry about. The real issue hides in the unconscious and has little or nothing to do with what they call "social justice" which is no more than a handy trigger to surface and explode much older and unrelated rage. Their demands give away the game. Demanding free education, free medical care, equitable distribution of wealth and on down a bottomless litany of complaints are the expectations of children, legitimate for little kids, inappropriate for adults, disastrous for society.

Are we also dealing with spoiled rich kids who never learned the value of responsible meaningful work and now misdirecting toward the wider world the anger they should have directed at their overindulgent, absent or negligent parents?

Acknowledging the uncertainties endemic in our tenuous grasp of reality does not justify resignation, but resolution to embrace the endless quest for truth. The ancient Greek sophists who preached relative truth and subjective reality have risen from the grave, invaded our educational system, preach social constructs, relative truth and a litany of other absurdities and risibly call themselves "progressives." That not so laughable sick joke falls on all of us in the form of an enormous but deliberately obscured ruinously expensive fraud.

We could examine the entire leftist body of thought, invert all the rationalizations, reverse all the conclusions and wind up with a fairly reliable recipe for social health. Mistakes would be few and minor. Leftist ideas have brought grievous harm rationalized with a belief in inverted justice, whereby people get what they do *not* deserve instead of what they should.

An ironic part of the fraud surfaces in people who keep telling us that we can't know anything for certain but nevertheless declare with certainty that the socialist variant of statism, with its very long historical string of lethal failures, is the only remedy for our political ills. They cloak deceit behind self flatteries.

I'd relish witnessing a quiet unheralded rebellion against the media-amplified noise coming from our culture haters who propagate the miasma emanating from our universities and vandalize monuments to honorable people who have contributed so much value to our legacy.

I repeat my favorite aphorism, "Reality will eventually reassert itself, but not before decades of political upheaval have destroyed the nation of people who defied it."

Small children at play show us the quintessence of human beings: playful, spontaneous, guileless, curious, wondering, lovable and trusting until indoctrinated adults pour every imaginable irrational notion into their little heads and corrupt their innocence.

And the result? Enraged college kids, who have not a clue to the source of their rage, screaming *fascist* and *racist* at ideas and people who contradict their indoctrination. K through PhD education is cheating our young people and imposing huge costs for the "honor."

What most non-science subjects focus on amounts to a gigantic fraud, its victims are young impressionable minds, the future of our nation, indoctrinated with a deluge of inanities just at the time of life when bright minds desperately quest for meaning, autonomy and truth. And all this emanates from the institutions charged with the vital task of enlightenment.

If ever there was a compelling argument for the separation of State and Education, it stands naked before us. We must reject tax funded education of any kind whatever, no departments of education federal or state, no government aid to schools, colleges or student loans, and no tenure laws. Zero, with not the slightest compromise that can and will start the cancer invasion over again. K-12 teachers and college professors must work directly for those who pay their salaries, that is, their students and funding parents, with no bureaucrats polluting the process. Such a policy would burden a great many people, but not worse than what young people now must endure.

An uncoerced market among providers and clients, whether in education or any other vital need, will inevitably attract profit-seeking inventors of gadgets and methods to increase learning availability and efficiency and reduce costs, a formula that many times has proven its value.

I exclude from this critique those who love to teach and not so enthralled with some religious or political doctrine as to prevent them from instilling a respect for autonomous inquiry and an honest search for truth in the young minds entrusted to them.

What clearer example could we hope for to illustrate the process by which democracy destroys itself than the present moral and political upheaval in this country? Voters are *choosing* the destroyers of our incomparable nation.

We will argue heatedly about the identity of the destroyers, what exactly is being destroyed, whether or not its destruction is justified, or whether or not its destruction will guarantee a better society. But scarcely can we argue that we are doing this to ourselves through the ballot box.

Some voters prefer one type of society, others promote another totally incompatible structure. Must the choice come down to the relative strength of the contending groups? Or should some inviolate principles decide the argument?

Everybody claims a hold on the truth usually embodied in their respective beliefs. The essential missing principle in the endless contentious efforts to impose one's version of the truth on everybody else is respect for the flawed but unfortunately only means we have to discover it.

Our present technology, most pertinently our capacity to destroy the world, has far outrun our self-understanding. A more dangerous specter confronting the human race is difficult to picture.

Our need to commit to the pursuit of truth and embrace reality to the extent we can has grown to a *literally* desperate life or death imperative. The questions raised by the Greeks two and a half millennia ago now confront us and can no longer be procrastinated. Our hour has come.

NOTES

1 https://nsba.org/-/media/NSBA/File/nsba-letter-to-president-biden-concerning-threats-to-public-schools-and-school-board-members-92921.pdf
2 https://news.yahoo.com/loudoun-county-mom-says-6-143637266.html
3 Commonly known locally as CU
4 Jacques Derrida, born in Algeria, was a French philosopher best known for developing a form of semiotic analysis known as deconstruction, which he analyzed in numerous texts, and developed in the context of phenomenology. — Wikipedia

MADISON'S ANGELS

WHEN HILLARY CLINTON WON THE POPULAR VOTE but lost the 2016 election, many political commentators joined an ever louder chorus of protest against what they see as an outrageous injustice built into our Constitution. Dating back more than a century, the chorus has criticized that venerable document as long outmoded, an ironic observation considering that these critics prefer collectivism, another name for tribalism that dates their ideas to the stone age. They decry the Constitution as anti-democratic, reserving their sharpest barbs for the Electoral College because it chose Mr. Trump over Mrs. Clinton, defying the popular vote. Many of these people also call for a proportionally elected unicameral legislature, that is, no Senate, and demand that our Constitution must become a living document that changes with evolving political circumstances.

These claims echo the past. Presidents Woodrow Wilson and both Roosevelts were contemptuous of the Constitution because it stood in the way of their "progressive" agendas. They, and many people since, preferred what has come to be called a "living constitution" that meets the needs of the present. A constitution subject to the whims of voters in a direct democracy with universal suffrage would qualify for little more than scrap paper. The term "Living Constitution" is a transparent attempt to send that venerable document to the guillotine and replace it with the caprice of the month.

"Another point which seems to me so basic that it is hard to grasp why there should be any argument is that law is virtually meaningless unless its principles are known in advance and can be relied on. Do judges have any sense of the amount of uncertainty and hesitation they create among decision-makers in all kinds of institutions, all across the country, when they ad-lib their decisions? People hesitate to expel hoodlums from school, to fire incompetents from work, or to do a thousand other things that need to be done, because nobody knows how some judge will apply the 'evolving standards' of a 'living constitution.'"[1]

An article in the *New York Times*[2] accused the framers of subversion, suggesting some clandestine and evil intent. The framers did not *subvert* democracy with some sneaky subterfuge, but were well aware of its troubled history, openly discussed its obvious shortcomings and deliberately built into our Constitution its characteristic separation of powers, numerous Congress-shall-nots, enumerated rights and a difficult revision process specifically designed to mitigate and dampen the momentary emotional hysterias that destroyed past democracies. They also wanted to give all states the same vote in the Senate so that the government would not be dominated by populous states.

The Constitution is an honorable document under dishonorable assault. The framers wanted a democracy constrained by difficult-to-change rules. James Madison's statement in Federalist #51 is revealing in this context, "If men were angels, no government would be necessary. If angels were to govern men, neither external nor internal controls on government would be necessary." Men notoriously are not angels. Hence the vital need to design a nation-defining document that would hopefully at least mitigate the iniquities common to a self-governing population.

Assuredly this is not the critics' intent, but their contempt for the Electoral College actually reinforces the present vital need for the very political document that they denounce.

The deep flaw in democracy stems from a root flaw in humanity. Humans are manifestly not angels, suffer from profound ignorance about themselves, cling tenaciously to risible beliefs as if life depended on them, and are capable of and often commit heinous offenses against themselves and others. The ignorant many far outnumber the enlightened few but possess the same individual voting power and overwhelmingly vote for welfare statists. Small wonder that statists love direct democracy and agitate to undermine the founding fathers' salutary efforts to mitigate the abuses of popular voting.

Why do statists praise and pretend to love democracy? Because they can control it to the benefit of the statism they profess. Why do you suppose that they pretend to champion the alleged downtrodden and encourage them to vote? Because such people believe themselves entitled and usually vote for public relief. If they did not vote for life at others' expense, the prevalent hypocritical concern for "social justice" would fly out the window.

Direct democracy cannot work because nothing prevents voters from electing colluding demagogues who then establish a parental government that brings an endless progression of unearned benefits to the electorate at the expense of the most productive citizens, which eventually bankrupts the society both economically and morally and clears a path for an autocrat. Look at the end of Republican Rome for an instructive tragedy. We are not Rome, but as Mark Twain quipped, "History does not repeat itself, but it does rhyme."

The fatal flaws of democracy are revealed in too many people clamoring to be fed and led, too many demagogues eager to accommodate, and far too many people seduced by false claims of justice, compassion and progress to sufficiently understand what strangles them and mount an effective resistance. By that means does democracy self destruct. Yet it has outshone other tried political structures, a grim indictment of our political doctrines. That democracy might be the least bad among the alternatives must not blind us to its considerable society-destroying power.

Socialism cannot work because it degenerates into universal dependency, irresponsibility, helplessness real or feigned, impoverishment and eventual dictatorship.

Capitalism cannot work when it is so widely and deeply distrusted and hated for its real deceits and perceived unfairness while a collusion of envy and demagoguery ceaselessly strives to bring it down.

Autocracy has not worked because the overwhelming number of bad kings, emperors and tyrants have bankrupted the industry and commerce over which they ruled; and throttled, dispossessed or murdered dissent. History has given us innumerable examples.

Theocracy, such as that ruling Iran, cannot work because it cannot tolerate deviation from absurd doctrines founded on myth.

Oligarchy, such as that ruling China, likewise cannot tolerate dissension and deviation from its clique's delusions of superiority.

Anarchy cannot work because the afflicted society has collapsed into a chaos of war lords, gang leaders and thugs all bent on pillage, rape and murder. Honest people can accomplish little else but defense of family, self and property, if that much.

A mixed economy cannot work because it is bitterly contentious with its numerous factions interminably contesting for power to impose their respective doctrines.

What does that leave? The Constitution of the United States of America, the checks and balances built into it and the nation it defines. Not perfect of course, for perfection depends on perfect people — angels Madison whimsically called them — and those we will never have. But it is the best we have so far in our world's unhappy history. Those who would supplant it with some version of direct democracy will most assuredly bring us something far worse.

The ideas that inspired the Constitution are more valid now for the preservation of freedom than when that incomparable document was adopted. It is worth fighting for and that means resolute opposition to those who will eviscerate it, who equate individualism with licentiousness and work to undermine this historically incomparable nation with seductive promises of a free life and vilification of alleged exploiters.

Against those who would destroy it, we must defend a vital but vulnerable document that deserves our respect and allegiance for standing as a barrier against despotism for well over two centuries. The founding fathers were far more enlightened and understanding of people than today's dystopians who agitate to destroy a unique Constitution they clearly do not understand and are in a contemptible pursuit to trash that noble document and establish universal larceny as a moral ideal.

After a thousand centuries of unceasing struggle against tribal, religious and political authority, a codified concept of the sovereign individual at long last enjoyed a brief time in the sun courtesy of the United States Constitution. Now statists eagerly shove that hard won gain back into the shadows with militant protests of the offense of the month.

Given our flawed nature, democracy is the best of the many political structures we have tried, but to survive it needs the circumscribed restraints of our Constitution.

Interminably contentious democracy is not the fault of evil people or the unenlightened voters in that political party you don't like, but attributable to the human condition that we all share, you and I included.

The striving to make democracy work falls on the shoulders of all of us. The applicable principle on which to model our actions has been developed as the methodology of science: observation, hypothesis, experimentation and verification, all resting on an inveterate respect for un-cherry-picked evidence whether or not that evidence reinforces one's cherished beliefs. In this vital process belief is the entrenched enemy whether theistic or secular such as the socialist myth promulgated in its numerous iterations by those who view parental government as the remedy for perceived social injustice and personal inadequacies.

The scientific method, so painfully developed over centuries, applies as much to human behavior and mental processing, although more easily perverted, as to the phenomena of the physical universe. We must dedicate ourselves to a rational but daunting pursuit of truth, a quest impossible or absurd to those who smugly imagine that their respective ideology holds all the answers or scorn the effort as an illusion.

Collusions of religious and political authorities have had their millennia. Demagogues with their reassuring certainties and seductive promises have had their centuries. All have left us a ghastly mess of history. Perhaps the time has come to give rational and responsible individual sovereignty a try? How could that be worse? Do we have the option to wait for Madison's angels?

NOTES

1   Thomas Sowell, *A Man of Letters*, Encounter Books, NY, 2007, p240
2   August 9, 2018

THE CONFLICTED REPUBLICAN PARTY

THAT THE REPUBLICAN PARTY finds itself in a serious internal conflict should be evident to anyone familiar with current political trends. But the question *why* proves much more elusive, and to my mind no one has come close to answering it. I attribute the source of that trouble to the Party's failure to affirm and actuate with sufficient force and conviction its own ostensible moral principles. Most damaging of all was and is the GOP's adoption in diluted form the ideas that have brought grievous harm to this incomparable nation.

We can without cynicism dismiss Mr. Biden's appeal for unity as a thinly veiled demand for cooperation with his statist agenda that he sees as just and proper. Republicans are labeled reactionary, backward and every other manner of denigration when they so much as question legislative proposals touted as "progressive" and "liberal" that are in practice the opposite.

Conservatives have come close to destroying themselves by repeating their opponents' self flatteries, promoting policies no more than diluted versions of what they claim not to like, inveighing against communism and socialism with little in the way of explaining why these trends are deleterious, and all the while clinging to doctrines as irrational as those they claim to detest. They have made themselves irrelevant.

Republican commentators and candidates base their assertions on little more than religious doctrines that have been under relentless and successful assault for centuries, then make the deadly mistake of constantly repeating their antagonist's pretentious self flatteries and conceding the high moral ground to the harmful ideas advocated by their alleged opposition.

A long line of republicans past and present have proposed nothing meaningfully different from that of the democrats they vilify. They thereby endorse the parental government principles advanced by their opponents. This tedious drama brings to mind Barry Goldwater's 1964 campaign slogan, "A choice, not an echo." Republicans ceaselessly echo, which is why they are perennially on the defensive. By all appearances Republicans haven't the foggiest notion of what they are up against.

Imagine yourself living in Western Europe in the early 1940s. The Gestapo hammers on your door and asks if you are hiding Jews in your attic. You and I would most likely agree that a lie would be a morally justified and praiseworthy act in the event that you were in fact harboring innocent refugees fleeing a lethal menace.

Now change the scene not all that much and imagine yourself inveterately committed to some religious or political belief. The leaders of your doctrine assure you that lying is justified and moral if it advances the cause of your shared beliefs toward their eventual global triumph.

Do you see a problem with the second scene? Because it lies (pun intended) at the heart of our present political acrimony. Islam and communism teach this as a moral tenet, and it is implicit in much current controversy.

Every side in our bitter culture war accuses every other side of lying and they are all, or most all, correct. Does anyone really pay much attention to the veracity of his or her assertions when they conform to an impassioned belief? Can a lie ever be justified on the pretext of advancing some doctrinaire cause?

To elevate the nature of this contest, the interminable conflict between republicans and democrats must refocus on moral principles, not just arguments about the degree of proposed policies. To answer the claim that "it's gone too far," what does "too far" mean? If a lot of something is bad, what makes a bit of it good?

Suppose you accuse someone, with whom you strongly disagree, of bias. He or she might reply or think, "Yes, of course I am biased, but biased to advance truth, justice and freedom. I do not think of myself as biased, but committed to what is right, fair and good. If some people see this as a bias, then I am biased and proud of it."

A committed believer would likely be contemptuous of an accusation of bias and proud of adherence to principles perceived as just and noble. Ideology trumps the search for truth, or to put it another way, respect for truth dies as dogma's orphan by abandonment. Believers have no need to search for truth since they have already found it embodied in their ideology.

We are all biased. We all have a preferred worldview. The American news media have for decades been accused of "liberal" bias, which is manifestly true, but the accusation misses the main act in the drama because the accused accept the rebuke with amused contempt for presumed moral inferiors. This is common among all doctrinaires. An accusation of bias will most often have the contrary effect than the one intended, that is, pride instead of shame.

Promoters of welfare statism see no harmful bias in their political advocacy, but rather include themselves among the morally righteous. Convinced that theirs is the only correct concept of a just society, they use any means fair or foul to bring that view into being. They fancy themselves as the progressives, the liberals, the just, the compassionate, the avant-garde, the politically correct. Their critics are biased, reactionary and live in the past. They see justice as egalitarianism, and any societal structure that permits huge disparities in wealth as unjust and must be overthrown. Although enjoying a superficial emotional appeal widely shared by republicans, very little deeper thought exposes this view as a widely prevalent fraud masquerading as progress, justice, freedom and truth. No greater deceit has been perpetrated against Americans and indeed the world.

The preponderance of intelligent leftists among college professors in part derives from their contempt for the obsolescence of the religion that they correctly associate with conservative republicans. But every bit as refractory as the people they treat with condescension, they refuse to recognize that the statist religion to which they adhere is the major source of worse absurdities, at least equally ancient and demonstrably far more dangerous.

When considering the appalling adversities that people have to endure in life and the many and hugely variant human inequalities perceived as unfair, the near universal yearning for a benign paternal government supported by widely accepted moral presumptions is not difficult to understand. But is such a political structure moral or even good for us? Grief and desperation reify myth.

For decades voters have clearly demonstrated that they want a parental government to at least mitigate the brutality and brevity of life and have persistently voted for demagogues who promise those benefits funded with purloined wealth rationalized as social justice and vilification of those relieved of their hard-earned money.

As has become evident, a majority of voters will never surrender their presumption of entitlement no matter the cost. What further self inflicted agony must the world endure before people finally get it into their heads that what they want is not possible? Their centuries-long attempts to realize that unfulfillable dream has piled up corpses and filled rivers of blood and tears, most tragically in the twentieth century.

The people who most loudly foster this dystopia are the same people whose socialist ideas have brought us Marxism, the most economically failed and lethal doctrine in history, whose related ideas have resulted in paragons like Soviet Russia, Nazi Germany, fascist Italy, communist China, North Korea, Venezuela, Cuba and smaller cells of hell, who brought us the bloodiest most grievous century in history, the twentieth, who scream *fascist* at people they don't like, who rationalize converting the streets of San Francisco into open sewers - a common source of deadly disease in medieval cities, who teach vulnerable young American minds that theirs is the worst country in history when in fact it is the best even with all its faults, who corrupt the meanings of justice, freedom, honor and truth, who have the effrontery to look down their insolent noses at "backward" republicans, then have the gall to call themselves liberals and progressives. Liberal and progressive in what way? Liberal with other people's money? Liberal with calamitous ideas? Progressive like driving toward moral and fiscal bankruptcy? Progressive like cancer advancing toward the destruction of its host? Progressive as in worming their way into the conduits of information to implant incremental advances toward the socialist mirage that has never failed to fail?

Karl Marx declared, "Religion is the opium of the people." His opiate has killed tens of millions of people. This is progress?

Hypocrites who readily slap *fascist* on those who disagree with them are evidently confused about the meaning of the word and should consult the man who coined it. Mussolini summarized fascism as, "All within the state, nothing outside the state, nothing against the state." Since leftists want the government to run everything including everyone's life, take parental care of everybody, and their kind to run the government, that would unmistakably make them the fascists.

These simple-minded people who see people as either oppressors or victims, presume moral superiority while advocating the most catastrophic ideas in history. Has a greater deceit ever been perpetrated against human happiness and flourishing than the innumerable frauds of socialist mythology? Thoughtful people, such as Republican Party members claim for themselves, cannot help but wonder what their condescending critics *really* want. Certainly not justice, social or any other kind. Their assertions and actions look more like disguised envy and malice coupled to a vindictive craving to control better minds.

The left has stolen yet another ancient device from religion to assure compliance with its doctrine, the guilt whip. For centuries believers have been told that they inherit "original sin" and consequent misery for the ludicrous rationalization that Adam and Eve ate a forbidden apple. Forever after people have been damned as impious sinners, corrupt, greedy, selfish and insensitive to the poor. Now, assert Marx's statist partisans, we are racist, fascist, unjust, avaricious and insensitive to the needs of the poor and disadvantaged.

The goals are the same:

- Enforce unquestioned obedience to presumptuous authority
- Bow heads in submission to inanities

- Silence opposition
- Eviscerate pride in achievement
- Give the perpetrators of this perennial fraud what envious and risk-averse people want: to entertain their shared delusion of a wiser grasp of reality and rule those who create, innovate, produce, accomplish, and bring value and true progress to the world.

The accusation that religious conservatives cling to ancient myths gains support from relentlessly expanding evidence, while their smug lefty critics adhere to a myth with a much worse murderous history. To which group would you assign the greater absurdity?

The meek shall inherit the Earth just like the myth claims. The intelligent, independent, responsible, rational, truth seeking, honorable and industrious must go somewhere else to be free to strive toward their dreams unencumbered by innumerable irrational rules drafted by smaller minds. Those left behind will elect demagogues making duplicitous promises that they have no ability or intention of fulfilling while they lead the masses to an un-mythical hell.

As we slowly catch up to European statism, we will like them, supplant our supernatural religion with a much more dangerous political one.

Republicans are ironically guilty of the accusations of injustice hurled at them by their critics. The injustice is against themselves when they accept abuse from, and repeat the self flatteries of, their markedly moral inferiors who pretentiously hold the high moral ground by default.

Reflect for a moment on a familiar biblical passage:

"Therefore I tell you, do not be anxious about your life, what you will eat or what you will drink, nor about your body, what you will put on. Is not life more than food, and the body more than clothing? Look at the birds of the air: they neither sow nor reap nor gather into barns, and yet your heavenly Father feeds them. Are you not of more value than they? And which of you by being anxious can add a single hour to his span of life? And why are you anxious about clothing? Consider the lilies of the field, how they grow: they neither toil nor spin, yet I tell you, even Solomon in all his glory was not arrayed like one of these." - Matthew 6:25-34

This statement, and similar absolutions, come not from "your heavenly Father" but from the father of woe. Mankind's countless rationalizations to dump the burdens of life onto supernatural and temporal authorities prevail as our perennial curse. And by the way, the "birds of the air" and the "lilies of the field" work very hard for a living according to their kind.

Try not to be concerned about "what you will eat or what you will drink, nor about your body, what you will put on" and see what happens to you.

The viable choices before us are not between an alleged unfair distribution of social status or a mirage of social justice, but ceaseless struggle or decay, enlightenment or ignorance, edification or demoralization, a relentless quest for truth or submission to reassuring myth, acceptance of responsibility or rule by charlatans.

Self-understanding has grown into our most pressing need, that followed by building a rational and secular foundation on which to rest moral principles. That rules out theism and statism. If the violent and doctrinaire idiots give them time, our most penetrating and honest thinkers will gradually evolve those most desperate needs.

Can any two committed minds ever reconcile their differences? The great majority of people would not so much as contemplate such an effort let alone think it necessary. I cannot imagine such a process outside of a successful psychotherapy — my own experience.

A related and dangerous developing phenomenon is once again rearing its ugly head carrying a specter of war hanging over humanity.

The more intelligent committed believers in some theistic religion, well aware that their beliefs do not accord with rational thought, nevertheless convince themselves that their faith rests securely on some "higher" reality beyond the reach of earth-bound science. Kant's separation of noumenal and phenomenal worlds and Gould's "non overlapping magisteria" furnished rationalizations for this shifty evasion of the rigors of rational thought.

Leftists have no need for rationalizations. They cannot or refuse to see that their worldview mirrors all the characteristics of a religious orthodoxy. They see no bias in what they believe to be true, nothing to examine or question. They eagerly apply any means fair or foul to reify their vision. That makes them particularly dangerous.

Picture the specter of a political religion like communism, fascism or some other variant of the socialist corpus, now armed with nuclear or pathogenic bombs as instruments of persuasion to enforce their orthodoxy on that part of humanity still unconvinced of the righteousness of the imposing doctrine.

Consider that the escape of the corona virus was an accident and not a heinous test by the Chinese Communist Party. Accident or not, the Chinese government cannot help observing the worldwide paralysis caused by the virus and give them cause to wonder if this might be an effective way to expand their power throughout the world.

Even wars do not settle differences. The losing side admits no error, only bitterly resigned to their defeat and determined to try some new clandestine strategy toward ultimate victory.

I have to conclude from this sequence of thoughts that our inability to reconcile our differences is incompatible with the cataclysmic weapons at our disposal. Perhaps the survival of our species hangs on substantially improving that incapacity toward much greater intelligence and understanding of ourselves.

I am very sorry that no one out there has all the answers. We might find one or two answers among leftists, but at the moment none come to mind. A few drift about within the Republican Party but with no in-depth understanding, usually only a not-so-subtle nostalgia for a religious resurgence.

I am afraid that trapped in the present stratum of understanding ourselves, we'll have to dig for answers. Effort is required and that requirement will hold for any future stratum of understanding in which we find ourselves.

We stumble along on an unsustainable course. We bankrupt the nation, erode the value of the dollar, bloat the government, promote the career of a future dictator, foster generations of dependent and irresponsible people, teach young people that goodness and truth are relative social constructs and ruinously charge them for the humbug. We allow vulgarians to defame and tear down our venerable heritage, invert the meanings of words vital to understanding freedom, unjustly burden and demean the productive self reliant people on whom a healthy society heavily depends, and at the base of all this rest our moral principles on foundations of theistic and political mythologies.

Conservatives, when will you get angry? Why are you allowing our destroyers to claim the high moral ground by fraud and default? Their fraud, your default. Conservative writings so often resemble chanting mantras in a wimp chorus expecting a magic force to sweep away the liberals. Do not fight this war — and war it most assuredly is — in the place where the enemy wants to confine you. Come out of the bilge where the culture pirates prefer argument by invective, mass disturbance and shouting insults at speakers they don't like. Climb up on deck and into the sunlight. Seize the ship, reset the sails to catch a stronger wind, set a course for a healthier and happier shore.

Grab the cannonballs that the enemy scorns: objectivity, probity, clear diction and evidence-based rationality, and attack their febrile gobbledygook. Load the cannons and blast away at the surrounding enemy with the precision of a marksman.

Do not collude with their deceit by calling them "liberals" and "progressives," or repeat their self-flattering adjectives and pretentious appellations like "well meaning" or political "scientists." These people are not liberal except for their profligacy with other people's money, and their collectivist ideas and herd mentality belong not to the future but to the tribal Pleistocene. They are *statists*. Label them with that dishonorable word.

We all know people who attach these labels to themselves (except stat-ist), and whom we consider well meaning. But well-meaning people can nevertheless create great harm. The well-meaning Fabian Society of England and others like it elsewhere and since have succeeded beyond their wildest dreams. Instead of bringing us the happier and more just world that they claimed to want, they have brought us to the brink of undiluted statism. Good intentions count for nothing if they drag us along a road to a hell on Earth. Do humanities professors mean well when they indoctrinate their students with hatred for Western Civilization?

Get angry! Your adversaries have earned your outrage for bringing so much harm to this country over so many decades. You have not earned their oft expressed contempt. Your outrage must become an admixture of the subtle, the indirect and the satirical to impart incisive punch to your words.

Our very difficult long-term goal must be to flush these people out of their redoubts in our universities, news media, cinema and government. The typical American university has become a perverse asylum, especially in the humanities. The nuts run the place and the sane, most of them in science, engineering and math, are cloistered and silenced with a politically incorrect toxin that they do not know how or want to fight.

Start building a rational *secular* foundation for morality based on indi-vidualism, reason and hard empirical science.

Get rid of the National Endowments for the Arts and the Humanities and other tax funded leftist propaganda effluents.

Go after the people who have been throwing acid in the face of our nation's Constitution (the document and the structure) for decades. *There* is where you should be aiming your heavy artillery.

And now for many of you comes the hardest part. You must accomplish all of this without reference to religion either explicit or implied. I do not expect that you would want to abandon your religion. Just keep it out of your arguments. It no longer persuades.

Strip away superstition, mythology, irrationality and the supernatural from religion and possibly we have a secular foundation of morality right in front of us. Religion has had the benefit of countless millennia of trials and errors to establish moral standards, many but not all of them good. We can think of this as empiricism applied over immense time. We don't kill, we don't torture, we don't steal, we don't lie, we don't cheat, we don't *initiate* force against others. Can we at least agree on that much?

It will not be easy to tell a majority of voters that their indoctrinated concept of social justice is not only *un*just, but the impelling cause of this historically incomparable nation's toboggan slide toward a precipice of no return. But if the statement is true, and I see it as such, then it becomes incumbent on principled people to convince listeners and readers of its truth by any honest, rational and respectful means possible, a task that faces a formidable but not invincible entrenched worldview. The political cancer from which we suffer has metastasized throughout the national body from its initial foreign invasion into the Northeast. Incrementally excising the malignancy demands a clear understanding of the cause of the sickness, effective remedies, dedicated opposition, perseverance and time. It cannot be done with either statism or theism, the reigning gospels of our time.

What is true? Do you care whether or not something is true? Or are you inveterately committed to your beliefs no matter what? Or have you so fused your faith with truth as to make them one and the same, a mistake shared with all doctrinaires including your disparagers whether theistic, political, social or personal?

As a species we stumble about in the dark groping for truth. Our better thinkers, recognizing their vulnerability to emotion-ruled conclusions, search more honestly. Others imagine that their beliefs have captured reality. Very few acknowledge that universal truth lies beyond our present capacity to comprehend.

A precious few intrepid and honest explorers creep up Mount Knowledge grimly aware that Truth snickers at and teases them from hidden crevices scattered all over the mountain.

FEMALE FEELINGS

I NDULGE ME FOR A LITTLE WHILE in a thought experiment. Momentarily suspend your initial reaction while considering the following idea.

A near universal cliché and a common joke among men has persisted for uncounted centuries that women are ruled by their emotions. Their reasoning ability is considered inferior to that of men … according to men. Most cultures throughout history have reduced women to second class citizens admired only for their beauty, charm and sexual pleasure, and fit only for domestic chores and motherhood. They have not even been fully trusted in the last role as guides for post pubescent boys. The general assumption has been, they don't think, they feel. This attitude has reached a deleterious extreme under Islam.[1]

A prevalent assertion in the popular media maintains that women are under-represented in STEM fields because male prejudice prevents women from pursuing careers in those subjects. A less politically myopic examination explodes that claim.

Is there a gender gap in the fields of science, technology, engineering and math?

Absolutely. But when researchers get past the ideological ax-grinding and look at the actual data, they find a different story than the one told by most of the media.

The first myth is that women are absent from STEM fields. In fact, many regions of the STEM universe are increasingly dominated by women. Ladies earn more than 60% of bachelor's degrees in the health professions, psychology, and biology — and that's been true for nearly 50 years.

Where women are underrepresented is in engineering and computer science careers.[2]

The number of brilliant women who defied the cultural and sometimes legal, (for example, Poland) opposition of their time and excelled in the hard sciences and mathematics has risen steadily since the seventeenth century. What these women achieved in the face of powerful cultural and political prejudice and opposition, and in at least one case (Helen Taussig) debilitating personal handicaps, inspires us with exemplary lives of courageous perseverance, heroic by any measure of that word. The Appendix presents an impressive list.

If we examine only one very difficult STEM career, medical doctors, the data repudiates any claim that women suffer unfair discrimination from men. The trend representing the number of women who graduated from U.S. medical schools with MD degrees has risen steadily without a dip from 4,000 in the 1980-81 academic year to near 10,000 in the 2018-19 academic year.[3] Not only has the number increased but also the percentage of total MD degrees, reaching near parity with men in 2019-20, 10,278 men and 10,109 women.[4]

None of this is new. It has been written about countless times and supported with compelling data. But if we momentarily assume for the sake of discussion that the cliché has come from many observations over many centuries that female emotions always trump their reasoning, and that women overwhelmingly choose activities and careers that deal with life, especially people, and not the physical world such as physics and engineering, how might this condition have come about?

The evident conclusion from the data is that women decline to study physics, engineering and computer science not from external barriers or lack of ability, but lack of interest. They do pursue medicine, biology, psychology, biochemistry and related life sciences, all every bit as difficult as any other STEM subject. Women are not turned away from the difficulty of a subject, but the subject's distance from life in general and especially people. Why?

If we approach the question from an evolutionary perspective, several facts help support the observation. Without some major, if not impossible, anatomical changes to a woman's body, the birth canal and therefore the newborn's head cannot get any larger. Compared to other animals, women already give birth with great difficulty, pain, and in past centuries, death. Yet over the great expanse of time, the human brain has gradually grown larger along with its intellectual capacity. How then might the pressures of natural selection have operated to evolve a way around this serious limitation? A couple of quotations set the stage for the argument that follows:

> Bipedalism is a demanding and risky strategy. It means refashioning the pelvis into a full load-bearing instrument. To preserve the required strength, the birth canal in the female must be comparatively narrow. This has two very significant immediate consequences and one longer-term one. First, it means a lot of pain for any birthing mother and a greatly increased danger of fatality to mother and baby both. Moreover, to get the baby's head through such a tight space it must be born while the brain is still small — and while the baby, therefore, is still helpless. This means long-term infant care, which in turn implies solid male-female bonding.[5]

> In the 1920s, the Frenchman Émile Devaux and the Dutchman Louis Bolk found the mechanism responsible for the human brain's remarkable development. Independently, each discovered that man, in contrast to other primates, is not fully developed at birth. Man remains in the fetal stage far longer than other mammals do, and thus

remains highly receptive to learning. Neuroscience can now confirm this hypothesis. While the brain of all other mammals grows more slowly than the body after birth, in man it continues to develop for quite a while at almost the same pace as in the womb. In this way, the human brain grows to a size that substantially surpasses that of other primates. The cerebellum and the cerebral cortex in particular profit from this continued growth. And within the cerebral cortex, it is above all the regions that are important for orientation in space, musicality, and powers of concentration that continue to develop.[6]

Since the human brain begins life outside the womb in a much less developed state compared to its adult form than is the case with other animals, that immediately leads to the question of what part is so much less developed at birth. The part that evolved last, the higher centers of the cerebral cortex, the thinking brain, the reasoning brain.

What parent, and in my case grandparent, has not observed emotions in uninhibited intensity spontaneously erupt in these delightful little people along with their total lack of reasoning powers?

Who then is better able to resonate with, understand and meet the needs of a crying infant who has no means other than screams, rages, squirming or cooing to communicate wants or discomforts, and thereby enhance his or her chances of survival? The warm nurturing emotionally available mother, who in the historical period of our most pronounced evolutionary progress, was the stay-near-home caregiver? Or the pseudo-logical aggressive father with little tolerance for emotional outbursts and in any case gone much of the time trying to contribute to the support and defense of family and tribe?

A chemical bond between a mother and her young is strongly evident in most species, especially mammals. A human mother is also emotionally bonded to the child to whom she has given birth. Her readily expressed feelings and emotional method of communicating with her child has been nothing less than a survival development for children and therefore of the human species. Why would such a powerful survival advantage not evolve into a gene-determined attribute? It makes no difference if she chooses to give birth or not. Her emotionally charged interest in life and caregiving come out of her gene-determined nature that she cannot escape.

Another benefit had to evolve. She had to be alluring and sexually available to hold on to the father (usually) to support her and her children during the long nurturing years. Culture and religion-enforced marriage bonds developed for the same reason, a necessity that has not diminished with time.

Many feminists, ignoring the obvious, have angrily protested the status of women as sex objects. It has proven an enormous benefit to the survival of our species that men are powerfully attracted to women's bodies and their warm emotions.

A woman's emotional sensitivity, warmth, beauty, charm, proclivity for care giving and sexuality are the happy results of this evolutionary development and among her most endearing and alluring characteristics, absolutely vital to the survival of our species. Her ready emotions, which resonate so well with those of little children, have come along as corollaries and go a long way in explaining why she gravitates toward subjects that focus on life.

All one need do is look at the history of political leadership to destroy in a blink any notion that men are more intelligent or rational than women.

See the Appendix at the end of this book.

NOTES

1   For confirmation of this assertion, I strongly recommend books by Ayann Hirsi Ali, Wafa Sultan and Oriana Fallaci.
2   Kaylee McGhee White, *Washington Examiner*, January 14, 2020, page 10.
3   Association of American Medical Colleges (AAMC), Graduates of U.S. Medical Schools by Sex, Academic Years 1980-1981 through 2018-2019
4   Association of American Medical Colleges (AAMC), Table B-4.
5   Bill Bryson, *A Short History of Nearly Everything*, Broadway Books, New York, 2005, Page 557.
6   Richard David Precht, *Who Am I*, Translated from the German by Shelley Frisch, Constable, London, 2007, page 16.

THE ADOLESCENCE OF HUMANITY

WE STAND AT THE THRESHOLD of the adolescence of our species, not unlike that faced by every young individual daunted by the coming challenges and responsibilities of maturity. As a species we must leave behind our gods, reassuring certainties and sugar daddy governments for the same reason that an adolescent must leave behind the dependency and security of parental care, and accept responsibility as a mature thinking self-sustaining adult. Can we individually or collectively decline to accept that challenge without dire personal and social regression?

We are trapped in a transitional era of moral chaos brought about by the disintegration of religious beliefs that stretch back into prehistory. With traditional religious canons swept away, we face fundamental questions for which theism can no longer provide answers that concord with reality. Humankind finds itself in an evolutionary vestibule of semi consciousness and poor self-awareness, caught between the instinctive reactions of the animal world from which we came, and the profound wisdom of our mythical sages and seers.

What is right? What is wrong? What is good and what not? What is true and what not? These questions must leave the domains of doctrines, dogmas and ideologies and now face the brutal contests of trial and error. What additional grief and horror will accompany those trials we can only hope to endure. Our only triumphs must become heroic ones over our eternal enemy, ignorance.

The wistful memories, terrors and gods of our species' childhood we must allow to slowly fade behind us as we advance through the burdens, challenges and joys of maturity that Nature demands of all creatures as the price of survival. We must not displace the dying gods of our childhood with reassuring demagogic deceits.

Religion is fighting for existence. Atheists and skeptics throughout the ages have smiled at the theistic beliefs of their respective age while wary of the authorities' methods of dissuasion. Today the non-believer argues and snickers in the open, for the first time on the offensive. Science and the increasing self understanding brought about by psychology have placed a sword and a shield into the hands of the non-believer who must not now succumb to worse seductions from political sirens.

How many more generations or centuries must pass before humankind steps across that threshold to embrace the self-empowerment of maturity I cannot guess. Wondrous it would be if humanity's reach for enlightenment could at least include these understandings and achievements:

- There can be no pride of accomplishment while remaining a dependent child throughout life.
- The principle has been established that standing on one's own two feet is the rite of passage from child to adult.
- The accepted standard of justice has resulted in a political structure that expects every independent rational responsible adult to reach his or her potential with no involuntary help from anyone.
- Inability for whatever reason confers no entitlement. Small children are the only exceptions.
- Humanity's moral standard has become responsible independent honorable productive adults.
- People have found ways to express courage in many more ways than valor in war.
- People have reached a time without the specter of war hanging over them.

- Parental government amounts to nothing more than an attempt to perpetuate childhood and nourish the arrogance of political poseurs.

- Parental government is a harmful solution to a misunderstood problem.

- Parental government undermines individual pride and self satisfaction in accomplishing something difficult, valued, meaningful and creative.

- Principles of autonomy and responsibility have been inculcated into every individual mind such that demagoguery and tyranny became impossible and freedom no longer has to be periodically purchased with the blood and deaths of heroes. The courageous no longer have to pay the price for the harm brought by the malice, cowardice and acquiescence of others.

- Thoughtful contributing people have discovered means to ease the burdens of life, reduce pain, lighten disappointments and losses, and live longer in contentment.

- To thwart the malignant creep of statism where each incremental advance justifies the subsequent invasion, government has been reduced to a dangerous necessity, denied any parental role and severely confined to protecting the citizenry from human-caused violence and predation.

- Most people finally grasp the profound power that a child's genetic endowment and early experiences exert over the beliefs, attitude, choices and direction of the later adult. Those early impressions have much greater influence than later philosophical or political teachings.

- Attempting to understand a personality, specifically why she or he believes and behaves as observed, without examining that personality from infancy, is as futile as trying to understand advanced mathematics without a foundation of simple arithmetic.

- Our dependence on belief, a timeless source of comfort, solace and assurance, has long been our greatest obstacle to enlightenment.

- Original sin is a horrible concept. Teaching an innocent and trusting child that he or she is stained from birth can have no other purpose than to inculcate the first of a long string of guilt inducements designed to control the mind with harmful indoctrination.

- Courts prosecute political types responsible for subsequent fiscal harm whether or not they have left office.

- It has become impossible for people to vote for benefits that must be paid for by their descendants.

Somewhere along the line of evolution from our primate ancestors, the creatures that would eventually become us became dimly aware that death inevitably waited at the end of a short and brutal life. A source of solace and assurance became imperative. People had to have their gods, mythical certainties and life after death in order to endure life. Rationality exerted little power then nor does it yet.

How much greater would be the despair of suffering people if they believed that this vale of tears was all there is? If there were no loving God waiting for them on the other side of death who would finally bring happiness and make everything right? Is this not the near universal yearning from which religions have derived their claims and authority?

To address this perennial dilemma more realistically we must find ways to bring more meaning and happiness and much less sorrow to daily living.

Leftists believe they have found those means in the various iterations of their professed doctrine. But their answer has proven more terrible than what it proposes to displace. The dissemblers and bunglers who proclaim and orchestrate that doctrine are manifestly not gods and cannot promise an afterlife but have only brought yet more misery to this one.

Is this not the grim reality that mankind must face if we are ever to break free of our species adolescence, accept what evolution has brought us and deal with it as best we can with courage, resourcefulness, understanding and compassion for what we are, and whatever love we can give to one another?

Consider the possibility that human evolution has resulted in an ever widening gulf between those who apply the lessons and methods of science to understand reality, and those who cannot or won't. How might this ever more contentious division eventually resolve itself?

- Major qualitative improvements in the understandings and techniques of clinical psychology might lead us to a much deeper understanding of ourselves and the roots of our fears, beliefs and conflicts.
- A global catastrophe such as world war, asteroid strike, epidemic or ice age any one of which would force the surviving few to devote their every mental and physical resource toward survival. The weak, incompetent or indolent would perish not from lack of compassion from others, but because there would be no alternative.
- Human genetic engineering could well accelerate our advance against the boundaries of ignorance especially about ourselves.

Human genetic engineering has been a hot topic among thinking people in recent years, especially since the outbreak of the Covid-19 virus. It would likely be more readily accepted as an idea with enormous beneficial potential if it had not been putrefied by the Nazi catastrophe. The advent of genetic engineering has already fired the starting gun in a race between the benefactor and the malefactor, the visionary and the destroyer, the statesman and the tyrant, and the cries of religions, theistic or secular, trying to prevent mankind from stepping intrepidly into the future without those ancient reassurances.

As a species we might well be approaching the time when we have no choice, that is, fundamentally change or perish. The awe inspiring progress of technology has brought to us the capacity to destroy humanity or all life on our planet. Can anyone honestly claim that the progress of self-understanding has kept pace?

I have imagined a parallel between fairly common individual neurotic symptoms, ones I share, and the same symptoms spread over the entire population. Some people struggling to understand their own painful feelings, commonly of anxiety or depression, fail to understand that the source of their discomfort is a lifelong yearning for the ideal mommy or daddy who would have satisfied vital emotional needs. Perhaps the actual parent was cruel, cold, inattentive, rejecting or absent during the most impressionable and vulnerable months of very early life and no nurturing surrogate was available to compensate.

In helping a patient struggle through this difficulty, the task of a therapist centers on acknowledging the loss, empathizing with its debilitating emotional consequences and helping the patient to accept the irreversible loss as one of life's tragedies, but not life destroying.

Compensations can be learned, but the responsibility to act on them belongs solely to the sufferer. At first glance this appears as an injustice but can't be otherwise. Time cannot be reversed, or mistakes undone. Mommy or daddy cannot be reborn into an angel and make all the hurts go away. The therapist's role can be briefly summarized in a declaration, "I am very sorry that you have had to endure such an awful experience and that now you must grapple with the inevitable emotional pain. It is my task to help you learn to accept that loss and find ways to overcome grief with joyful living. Many possibilities lie open before you. I will help you identify them. Let's do this together."

Imagine now that the suffering patient is the entire nation and the therapist a sort of national political psychiatrist. The diagnoses of the maladies in the two cases do not differ all that much. The great majority of people yearn for an easier life with many fewer losses, disappointments, setbacks, sicknesses and griefs. Many of these same people feel entitled to compensation for their suffering, lesser abilities or less favorable circumstances.

The task of our hypothetical political psychiatrist is very close to that of the individual's case and can be briefly summarized in a similar declaration, "I am very sorry that you have had some pretty awful experiences, some of them inordinately grievous. But these difficulties need not be life destroying, can be at least partially compensated with more realistic and effective actions, and in any case do not entitle you to compensation from your fellow humans all of whom also struggle in some measure with life."

Whether you are left or right, liberal or conservative, collectivist or individualist is to me delusional and superficial. The task before us is not to find a way to elect the "right" politicians or build the "correct" political structure, but to find a way to break the chains that bind us to our first few years of life.

The political goal should be capitalism that finds a benign balance between thriving industry and entrepreneurial risk-taking on one hand, and sensitivity to the human condition that fosters independence and responsibility on the other. This ideal will never be achieved by establishing universal larceny and dependency administered by government.

GLUE?

CONVENTIONAL WISDOM MAINTAINS that eighty to ninety percent of our brains consist of glial cells, collectively called glia, a word derived from the Greek word for glue. The remaining ten or twenty percent, neurons, the focus of most current research into cognitive processing, are understood as the principal players on the stage of the brain's drama. Assigned supporting roles, glial cells presumably work out of the spotlight to assist neural functioning in some as yet poorly understood way.

The focus of this essay can be condensed to a simple question: Considering at the very least the economy of structure found everywhere else in biology, does it make any intuitive sense that Nature would fill eighty to ninety percent of our heads with cells that function only to serve the remaining ten to twenty percent?

The wizards and sages of our legends and folklore furnish alluring portraits of the powers of penetrating thought that many of us yearn to find within ourselves. Must we, like adults setting aside the toys of childhood, dismiss these stories as no more than amusing but irrelevant fables? Or do these universally appealing images lure us with some dimly perceived but forever receding potential of our minds?

We attempt resolutions of our interminable interpersonal conflicts with a curious lack of appreciation for the source and nature of the difficulty. Disagreements, whether between spouses or nations, or tormenting internal dilemmas faced alone, are rooted in if, what and how we think. And we think, if at all, with our brains. To ask the questions, "where does he or she get those ideas", "why do they differ from mine" or "why is it so difficult for each of us to see the other's viewpoint much less agree with it", logically leads to the more fundamental question, "how does the mind work?" But disagreements within the general public rarely inspire such considerations and the more heated the dispute, the further the adversaries fly from reflections about brain functioning except as derisive imputations of the others' lack of it. My own frustration with the obstacles to external, and especially internal, conflict resolution furnished the incentive for the thoughts and investigations that led to this essay.

Many baffling and intriguing questions inspire study of the brain. Since the latter half of the last century, we are beginning at last to think about thinking in unprecedented ways. Questions about how the mind works have drifted away from the philosopher's detached speculations and been brought under the empirical scrutiny of laboratory researchers and their ingenious instruments. The results so far will astound anyone with more than a superficial interest in the subject.

The more we learn about our marvelous organ of thought, the less it seems we know about it. Its myriad and baffling complexities expand before us, a labyrinth of passageways and doors leading to yet more passageways and doors, endlessly multiplying. Probed alive by machines a thousand times its size, poked with electrodes, dissected by pathologists, sliced in half while still alive[1], anesthetized, traumatized, and pondered by millennia of physicians, philosophers, mystics and quacks, the brain continues to elude understanding of itself by itself.

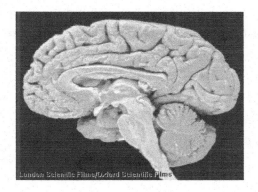

London Scientific Films/Oxford Scientific Films

As if this picture were not daunting enough, one of the more amazing discoveries of recent research is the brain's power to continuously create itself, that is, to form ever-changing networks of connections in response to environmental experiences and choices of the individual.[2] It's like trying to study a shape-changing creature from science fiction, at once marvelous and mysterious.

This is likely the principal non-genetic process by which small children form their personalities. The child's reactions to the home environment influence the formation of brain cell patterns, urging the development of some while atrophying others, both subject to limits imposed by genetic predisposition. That is also most probably why personalities solidify so early in life. Much of the brain's processing, and therefore thinking, becomes in a sense "hard wired".

Weighing about three pounds and sectioned into various ancillary organs, the brain contains about fifty billion nerve cells (neurons) and about twenty times that number of glial cells according to at least one count[3]. Another count raises the ante to one hundred billion neurons, each contacting ten thousand others and each capable of sending up to a hundred messages a second.[4]

Current research favors studying the electrochemical activities of neurons as the brain's defining business. The brain's sole activity might consist of billions of neurons sending impulses to one another, but this seems counterintuitive and probably prejudiced by our knowledge of computers and the relative ease of non-invasively measuring neural electrical pulses with ever-increasing sophistication. It's counterintuitive because neurons, the alleged collective essence of the mind, number only a small percent of glial cells.

So why all those glial cells?

According to most current research, the much more numerous glial cells do no more than insulate, separate and in some unknown fashion "help" the neurons, giving the brain a kind of structure similar to delicate fibers (neurons) suspended in stiff jelly (glia).

Early researchers likely did not know what to call that great mass of brain cells with no observable function. Observing the vigorous pulses of the much less numerous neurons have always furnished an easier focus of study. So, the far greater number of, but more obscure, cells were whimsically dismissed as a kind of glue holding the brain together.

Later research has so far identified several types of glial cells, some with neural supporting functions (nourishment, waste removal and insulation), and others still poorly understood but leaving subtle clues to a much more central importance.[5] The word *glial* has not only become an inappropriate adjective but obscures the multiplicity of dissimilar types and functions of these cells.

I am not a biochemical research scientist but would like to stimulate thought in the non-specialist population with a few simple questions. Are we to believe that Nature, parsimonious everywhere else, fills our heads with cells demoted to supporting roles collectively called glue? With considerable justification we may accuse ourselves of filling our heads with all sorts of junk, but glue has never featured high on the list. Does the bulk of the brain's cells exist solely to provide a structural matrix to hold in place, protect and assist the neurons in some yet unexplained way? Would such spatial inefficiency likely have evolved, given a development time measured in hundreds of millions of years?

At least a few researchers agree:

A view held by many neurobiologists is that the complexity of our behavior will ultimately be accounted for by simple interactions between neurons and glia. Whereas neurons interconnect to form electrically active circuits, the role of glia is a mystery. Do glial cells just provide a passive framework that supports, nourishes, and insulates neurons, or, in addition, do glial cells play more active roles in signaling and plasticity? The potential importance of glia is suggested by their increase in number during evolution; glial cells constitutes [sic] 25%, 65%, and 90% of cells in Drosophila [fruit flies], rodent, and human brain, respectively.[6]

Until recently, neuroscientists thought cells called glia were the nervous system's supporting players, helping keep brain cell communication in working order. Researchers focused more attention on the brain's 100 billion nerve cells called neurons. Recent studies, however, suggest glia play a vital role in brain cell communication, and perhaps in the development of human intelligence.

Cells known as glia (Greek for "glue") were long believed to provide nothing more than support to nerve cells. Research is showing, however, that glia are active participants in brain function.[7]

In the past, glia were understood to support neurons; to feed them and clean up after them, and to respond to brain injury. But these functions were regarded as peripheral to the exciting functions that neurons perform in processing information and storing memories. Consequently, research on glia did not fare well in the fierce competition for the limited grant funding for brain research. Neuroscientists were not trained in glial science, and the standard texts cover glia superficially, if at all. Editors at major journals were not well versed in these odd and very complicated brain cells. As a consequence, glial research was rarely published in high-impact scientific journals. These forces dragged on glial researchers for decades. Now all of this is changing.[8]

Synaptic plasticity is thought to be initiated by neurons only, with the prevailing view assigning glial cells mere specify supportive functions for synaptic transmission and plasticity. We now demonstrate that glial cells can control synaptic strength independent of neuronal activity.[9]

In an interesting study, the University of California counted the number of glial cells in a slice of Einstein's brain (preserved after his death in 1955) and discovered that he possessed many more glial cells per neuron than those counted in a control group of brain tissues.[10] That single example, derived from an examination of one of the greatest minds of the twentieth century, poses an intriguing question about the purpose of these cells.

Each age has contributed its notions of understanding the brain based on whatever technology seemed most impressive at the time. "The early Greeks . . . thought of mental processes in terms of the flow of bodily fluids. . . Descartes compared brain functions to the operations of machines. The nineteenth century emphasized anatomy . . ." and an early twentieth century thinker "compared brain operation to a telephone switchboard."[11] Today, computers furnish analogs to the brain that are probably just as misleading as previous attempts to explain the brain's complexity in terms of contemporary gadgetry.

We should see the brain not as computer, but as a wondrously complex electrochemical processor that functions at the ionic level. Ions (electrically charged atoms or molecules) move across cellular membranes called synapses and cause changes in receptor cells structured to receive and react to them. Research into brain activity must therefore focus on the infinitesimal. Although the brain is not a computer, developments with parallel distributed processing computers at least promise to furnish valuable insights into the brain's activity.[12]

Nerve activity is electrochemical. Long thin cells — one can't help but think of wires — carry electrical impulses, stimulated by electrochemical neurotransmitters, to every cell in the body. Nerve cells stimulate one another in a chain reaction analogous to the near instantaneous nuclear geometric expansion of an atomic bomb. But they also turn one another off lest the geometric progression of "firing" neurons (that's the term used) continue beyond the purpose of the firing pattern.

What starts neurons firing in some specific pattern? Why that pattern and no other? What starts a thought, an idea, a sudden epiphany, or the Olympian Majesty of Beethoven's ninth symphony? What stimulates a memory? How are memories stored and retrieved? What recognizes a face? What drives the artist, writer or inventor? Are we to believe that these marvels come from billions of neurons conducting electrochemical impulses to and fro? From where and to where? From where comes the initial stimulus that excites the first neuron to send an impulse on its way to spark a staggeringly complex process that we as yet so dimly grasp?

Is it possible that the thoughts, images, language, music, poetry and ideas correspond to patterns of firing neurons insulated by and immersed within a gelatinous mass of glial cells? Only a modest intuition aroused by a respect for Nature's efficient biology and a little curiosity about the purpose of all those cells taking up so much valuable space for so menial a task, cries out for a different direction of inquiry than the one pursued by a preponderance of contemporary research.

Suppose instead that cognitive activity originates in the misnamed glial cells in the form of chemical reactions analogous to those that occur within the neural synapses, and these initiate the impulses carried by the neurons. Accordingly, I suggest in place of at least one of the types of glial cells, most likely the astrocytes, the name *penson* (pen'sahn) which is derived from the old Latin *pensare*, to think[13]. Each penson would function as a tiny chemical factory. The movement of ions within a single penson could be unique to that type of cell, and/or the pensons could form communication networks with one another by virtue of their neural "wiring" or with adjacent cells via ion exchanges through cell walls.

As an analogy, imagine yourself working in an office within a high rise building and engaged in a teleconference call among a great many other people. Some occupy adjacent and nearby offices within the same department where you work. Others work up or downstairs in departments other than yours but with closely or distantly related functions that interact in some essential way with your function. Still others work in different buildings, even with different companies in different parts of the country, but who contribute essential information to the issue under discussion. Each person analogizes to a penson, each office wall to a penson cell wall, the telephone wires to neurons, the telephone handsets to synapses, the spoken words to ionic exchanges across the synapses and electricity through the phone wires to electrochemical impulses along the axons (the long fibers) of neurons.

This essay suggests the hypothesis that at least one of the types of misnamed glial cells, most likely the astrocytes, collectively *are* the brain and the neurons serve as their interconnecting wiring. It's a hierarchical inversion of the prevailing assumption that deserves further study.

If we could only widen the crack in our ignorance a little by first giving these enigmatic cells a bit more enlightened attention than they have so far received, and secondly by warily regarding computer models as currently fashionable red herrings, our investigations may lead to a watershed in our understanding of how we think, and therefore how we create, interrelate and argue with one another. A more thorough understanding of how we think will unquestionably lead to more congenial resolutions of contentious viewpoints because it will give us a better grasp of the development of views that contrast with our own.

I would like to think that if we can discover the nature of the brain's functioning, we can develop methods to remove at least some of the blocks to amity and wisdom and alleviate the life-robbing mental torments that plague our species.

CORROBORATIVE BOOKS

1. Andrew Koob, *The Root of Thought*, Pearson Education, Inc. FT Press, Upper Saddle River, NJ, 2009.
2. Alexei Verkhratsky and Arthur Butt, *Glial Neurobiology*, A Textbook, John Wiley & Sons Ltd. West Sussez, England, 2007.

NOTES

1 Done in a surgical procedure called a *corpus callostomy*.
2 Restak, Richard. *Brainscapes*, New York: Hyperion, 1995. p93. See also Norman Doidge, *The Brain That Changes Itself*, Viking, New York, 2007.
3 Restak p40.
4 Hobson, J. Allen. *The Chemistry of Conscious States . . .* (Boston: Little, Brown & Company, 1994) p28.
5 "Types of Glial Cells". http://lshome.utsa.edu/courses/Neurobiolab/Assign-03hist/html/glia.htm.
6 Barres, Barbara A. "Neuron-glial interactions". *Molecular and Cellular Approaches to Neural Development*. ed. W. Maxwell Cowan, Thomas M. Jessell, and S. Lawrence Zipursky. (New York: Oxford University Press, 1997) p64.
7 Susan Perry, *Glia: the Other Brain Cells*, BrainFacts.org, September 15, 2010.
8 R. Douglas Fields, *Glia: The New frontier in brain science*, Scientific American, November 4, 2010.
9 Anna K. Clark, Doris Gruber-Schoffnegger, Ruth Drdla-Schutting, Katharina J. Gerhold, Marzia Malcangio, and Jürgen Sandkühler, *Selective Activation of Microglia Facilitates Synaptic Strength*, The Journal of Neuroscience, March 18, 2015.
10 *The Infinite Voyage, Fires of the Mind*, video tape. (Van Nuys, CA.: Vestron Video, 1988)
11 Restak, Richard. *Receptors*. (New York: Bantam Books, 1994) p5.
12 Churchland, Paul M. *The Engine of Reason, the Seat of the Soul*. (Boston: The MIT Press, 1995) p11.
13 Current Latin dictionaries translate the English infinitive *to think* as *cogitare*. But that word does not slide into a nice sounding noun. The older Latin verb converts into a better noun and still survives in French *penser*, Italian *pensare*, Spanish/Portuguese *pensar* and Sardinian *pessare*.

AN INFINITY OF SPACE
AN ETERNITY OF TIME

E INSTEIN AND NUMEROUS ASTRONOMERS have speculated about this possibility long before I latched on to the idea. Picture the universe as incomprehensibly vast, perhaps infinite and eternal. I want to use that image as a metaphor to convey an idea.

If we consider only the observable universe, the one within reach of our instruments, the figure commonly cited is 13.7 billion lightyears in all directions.[1] That implies a sphere 27.4 billion lightyears in diameter with Earth at the center, a "pale blue dot" Carl Sagan called it. That immense volume of space is also expanding in all directions at an accelerating rate like an inflating balloon.

The vastness of the universe implies an equally vast reality, an equally vast number of truths, and further implies that the quest for the limits of truth can have no end. That in turn diminishes our present grasp of truth and our concepts of reality to the infinitesimal. It shrinks all of our reassuring certainties, dogmas, doctrines, religions and ideologies to comforting myths. Those who believe they have found *The Truth* in their theistic, political, social or personal religion are furthest from it. They cling to an illusion.

An inveterate ideology, dogma, doctrine or personal belief can rest on no firm foundation. Even the present compass of all human knowledge expands with new discoveries, especially in science, that emerge all the time and challenge long established truths. Considering the expanse of the universe, certainties must inevitably submit and often succumb to the test of reality.

Does that mean that scoffers, who, fearful of the unknown and shrinking from the daunting task of discovery, believe something worthy of our consideration? That we can know nothing? There are no truths? Truth is a social construct? Everything is relative to one's familial and cultural immersion? The search for truth amounts to a futile delusion?

But the scoffers suffer their own peculiar delusion.

The advance of knowledge must be provisional and contingent on future discoveries. We are stuck, whether we like it or not, with forming our choices and decisions while burdened under the disquieting fact that we might be wrong and advancing along the wrong course.

Nevertheless, we must deal with the trials, conflicts and vexing uncertainties that press upon us daily with little or no concern for what better understandings might arrive in the future. But could we at least recognize that our precarious hold on reality gives cause to question the beliefs, dogmas and certainties that command so much of our devotion and passion?

Picture the totality of reality as an immense body or blob of some sort out of which we take little bites now and then in our never-ending quest to discover meaning and truth. We collectively chew on the bites for a few decades or generations, then either spit them out or swallow them, integrating them with our current understandings. The better thinkers among us acknowledge the tooth-breaking uncertainties hidden in the bites.

Our grasp of reality, the truths on which we depend, are without doubt tiny. But tiny is not zero. Truths impinge on our senses from all around us in the natural beauty we behold everywhere and the wonders we create ourselves.

Allowing the scoffers to rule our minds betrays ten thousand generations of ancestors who were forced to learn those truths vital for daily survival and to understand their world as best they could, all the while armed with none of the knowledge and instruments of discovery available to us. Our knowledge, small though it may be, is commensurate with our present levels of understanding and cognitive capacity. The scoffers' contemptuous dismissal of the effort of thinking evades the struggle for truth that the more honest among us must continue indefinitely if we as a species are ever to achieve the self-ful-fillment, happiness and some measure of assurance for which humans have universally yearned throughout our tumultuous time on Earth.

This same universe metaphor applies to the analogous affirmation that free will is also a delusion. With our half animal minds and the unconscious but powerful influences that very early nurturing experiences exert over later adult behavior, we in consequence do not know ourselves all that well. But as with the nibbles we bite out of the totality of reality, the reasons we dream up to rationalize our beliefs, choices and actions are not entirely spurious. We do have *some* free will, the profound thinkers among us more than others, the span ranging from zero to very rare honest self-examination.

Certainty must suffer the fate of ineluctable doubt in the face of an incom-prehensibly vast reality and our limited cognitive capacity to comprehend that reality. That includes poor self-understanding of why we do what we do, the tap root of most or all human-created woe.

The solace and reassurance that we have always sought in our gods, reli-gions, beliefs and political doctrines we must surrender as illusions if we are ever to achieve inner freedom. Relief from the burdens, pain, responsibili-ties, grief and brevity of life — those yearnings that beat in the hearts of all of us — are what people want most and what demagogues, charlatans and political power types throughout the ages have deceitfully promised their listeners and readers. But we cannot escape life's tribulations until we escape life itself. What recourse does that leave us except to face those trials with whatever courage and resources we can muster?

Long before our unwanted end, we can discover or create compensating joys in the forms of a meaningful constructive purpose, courage to persevere, companionship, humor, edifying art, the awe of natural beauty, pondering the incomprehensible expanse of the universe; delighting in a child's curiosity, wonder, spontaneity and growing awareness; a day of happiness, a project well thought out and executed, the love we give to one another... now you add to the list.

The entire history of mankind is but an eye blink on the time scale of evolution. To imagine that biological evolution has reached its highest expression is absurd. As long as this or any other planet can harbor life, organisms of whatever sophistication from protozoan to sage will be *compelled* to relentlessly compete for food, living space and reproductive mates and defend against lethal threats of whatever kind or sophistication. Evolution is therefore natural, inevitable and good.

With the severe limitations in thinking manifested in our philosophically chaotic and contentious world, I assert that there exist truths about our immense and mysterious universe that lie beyond the present capacity of understanding even in our most gifted thinkers. Apprehending those truths must await an expansion of cognitive capacity. In the meantime, we can experience searching and discovery as unending adventures. The search for truth can be as inspiring and endless as the universe itself.

NOTES

1   NASA – The Hubble Telescope

A UNIVERSE OF CONCERTINAS

L ABEL THIS IDEA A conjecture, neither a belief nor a claim to certainty. Consider for a moment the universe — not a multiverse — as both infinite and eternal.

Astronomers have determined the distance to the edge of the observable universe at about 13.7 billion light years in all directions. *Observable* is a key word here. The unknowns that lie outside that observable sphere tease us with numberless possibilities for speculation. I offer one here.

That part of the universe that we can detect has been expanding at a great rate since the putative Big Bang started it all 13.7 billion years ago. Astronomers cannot be sure if the observable universe will go on expanding forever or reach some limit and start contracting again similar to the action of a concertina. To pursue this idea a little further, let's assume the latter.

Our observable expanding and eventually contracting universe might endure for tens of billions of years. We really don't know yet. But imagine that it is only one among an unknown but huge number of analogous concertinas each expanding or contracting in accordance with its own time cycle like independent islands in the limitless cosmos. If this idea has any merit, it would mean that the death of our sun, predicted a few billion years from now, would not necessarily extinguish the human species or any other that we might wish to preserve.

Carrying this idea still further, we know that many people profess a strong faith in God. Others demote God to "some power higher than ourselves." I do not without reservations accept either of these suppositions, but a universe of concertinas would satisfy either belief and rest them on a plausible foundation without recourse to the supernatural. Nor would the idea contradict our present knowledge of the universe.

Arthur C. Clarke once wrote, "A sufficiently advanced technology would be indistinguishable from magic." Expanding his statement, a sufficiently advanced species would be to us indistinguishable from gods. A region of the universe billions of years ahead of our cycle would have had sufficient time to evolve just such a species who could, as their cycle neared its uninhabitable time, never suffer extinction. They would move to another concertina in an earlier period of its cycle. This plausibly could determine the far distant future of humankind.

SEVENTY-THREE AND TWO

by Michael H. Davison

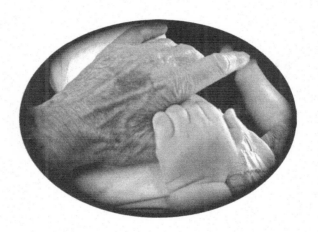

From age to guileless youth enjoined are we
To pass the gifts of life, love and mind.
How then shall we guide our lives
To conform with this decree
And leave a happier world behind?

Sage or fool? Producer or thief?
Healer, teacher or bringer of grief?
Builder, destroyer, seeker of truth?
Explorer, predator or mentor to youth?

What is true? What is just? asked the Greeks,
Then sent Virtue to the helm.
Which Virtue do we send to seek the truth
And to a place where honor speaks?

Courage, love, probity, perseverance?
Wisdom, beauty, composer of the sublime?
Have these not all been staged with endless praise
In poem, drama, song and eloquence
Only to suffer the cynics' flays?

Do we even know whom to send?
Liberal or conservative?
Left or right?
Socialist or capitalist?

Democrat or Republican?
Statist or individualist?
Believer or atheist?
Has thought not revealed itself
With more than two divisions to contend?
Our political rancor we must transcend
Lest another civil war brings our end.

Lies fly from every side
In our churlish culture war.
Truth's respect we've stultified
And civil discourse we abhor.

Deceivers debauched the word progressive,
As well the once honored name of liberal.
Their discourses argue by invective
While red flag of menace they unfurl.

Deconstructionists they call themselves
And append the flatteries just and fair.
Then add postmodernism
As if they owned the future air
They see no harmful bias in their deceit
And <u>that</u> is the hubris we must defeat.

A mask of justice hid universal larceny
When compassion became the tool hypocrisy.
Ours became the mendacious age
When duplicity ruled the game.
Treachery will lock us in a cage
To our lasting complicit shame.

How do we pose the rules of life,
Ones mainly free of strife?
Plant the good in nourishing soil
That ignorance cannot despoil
And safe from the cynic's scorn?
Must we wait for new knowledge born?
At what more cost in blood and tears?
Return to gods, priests and prayers?
What have we seen in history's gods
To assure a world where truth inheres?

We cannot return to trinities old,
Not Father, Son nor Spirit Holy
Nor faith, hope and charity.

Amity must a new trinity uphold
That Wisdom, Honor and Courage reign.
In Wisdom's soul good mind,
Knowledge and fair judgment be,
And honor we must ingrain.
Whence came you and me
And whence came our heritage
If not from ancestral courage?

Freedom's modes external and internal
Must come first in world and mind
Before virtues can have a home to find.
Freedom you claim in both modes?
You've challenged your personal codes?
Renounced the doctrinal straitjacket
That honest quests for truth upset?
Rules from daddy, mommy and teacher
No longer your mind beset?
Gods to youth's delusions fled?
No dogma label stuck to forehead?
Your prejudices discarded?

Relative truth rejected?
No emotion enervates?
No obsession subjugates?
No Pollyanna fantasy?
No either-or dichotomy?
Morality from caprice untethered?
A quest for truth trumps your ideology?
You refuse to see these two synonymous?

Tell me you comply with this advisory
And I'll ask you how you know.

What test will prove your psyche free
And no duplicity show?

Can anyone heed this stern advice?
Can anyone escape their childhood years?
The ones etched deep by fears and tears?
We to feelings' rule befell,
Ourselves we know not well,
Why we believe and behave as inclined.
To struggle in ignorance we are assigned
While Wisdom flees the troubled mind.

Justice, courage and compassion
Warp in a subjective mirror.
How brief our feeble hold on truth must last,
Yet how precious are those bits hard won
In a universe incomprehensibly vast.

Despite our inborn imperfection,
Forlorn child of the human condition,
To us falls an arduous task perforce,
Constant struggle must be our course
In which courage must persevere.
Before us boundless opportunities call.
Wonder and curiosity must not to apathy fall.
In honest pursuit of truth our minds must bend.
On neither theistic nor political guide depend.
The quest must be for me, not just for we.
Bow we must to this decree.
The quest for truth can have no end.

APPENDIX

NOTABLE BRILLIANT WOMEN IN SCIENCE AND MATHEMATICS

NAME	BIRTH	DEATH	COUNTRY	FOCUS	DATA SOURCE	Notes or Nobel Prize
Hypatia	360?	415	Greek Egyptian	Mathematics, Astronomy	RI	
Marie Cunitz	1610	1664	Poland, Germany	Astronomy	Noyce 1	
* Marie Meurdrac	1610	1680	France	Chemistry	Noyce 1	
Maria Winkelmann Kirch	1670	1720	Germany	Astronomy	Int	
Laura Bassi	1711	1778	Italy	Physics	Noyce 1	
Marie Gaetana Agnesi	1718	1799	Italy	Mathematics	Noyce 2	
* Marie Geneviéve-Charlotte	1720	1805	France	Botany, Biochemistry	Noyce 2	1
Caroline Herschel	1750	1848	Germany, England	Astronomy	Wiki	
Wang Zhenyi	1768	1797	China	Mathematics, Astronomy	RI	
Sophie Germain	1776	1831	France	Mathematics	Noyce 2	
Mary Somerville	1780	1872	Scotland	Mathematics, Astronomy	Wiki	
* Mary Anning	1799	1847	England	Paleontology	Wiki	2
Elizabeth Fulhame	17xx	?	Scotland?	Chemistry, textiles	Noyce 2	
Augusta Ada Byron	1815	1852	England	Mathematics	Noyce 1	3
Maria Mitchell	1818	1889	USA	Astronomy	Wiki	
* Florence Nightingale	1820	1910	Italy, England	Nursing, public health	Noyce 1	
Elizabeth Blackwell	1821	1910	USA	Medicine	RI, Int	
Elizabeth Garrett Anderson	1836	1917	England	Physician	JC	
* Mary Putnam Jacobi	1842	1906	USA	Physician, medical research	Noyce 1	
Emily Warren Roebling	1843	1903	USA	Engineering	RI, Int	
Sophie Kovalevskaya	1850	1891	Russia	Mathematics	Noyce 1	
Hertha Ayrton	1854	1923	England	Math, invention, electricity, sand ripples	Noyce 2	
* Nettie Stevens	1861	1912	USA	Genetics	RI, Int	
* Esther Lederberg	1922	2006	USA	Microbiology	RI, Int	
Florence Bascom	1862	1945	USA	Geology	RI, Int	
Marie Sklodowska Curie	1867	1934	Poland, France	Radioactivity	Noyce 1	4
Mary Agnes Chase	1869	1963	USA	Botany	RI, Int	
Ynés Mexia	1870	1938	USA	Botany	JC	
* Florence Rena Sabin	1871	1953	USA	Medical research, public health	Noyce 2	
Lillian Gilbreth	1878	1972	USA	Psychology, engineering	RI, Int	
Lise Meitner	1878	1968	Austria, Germany	Nuclear physics	Noyce 1	
Emmy Noether	1882	1935	Germany	Mathematics	Noyce 1	5
Edith Clarke	1883	1959	USA	Electrical Engineer	RI, Int	
* Karen Horney	1885	1952	Germany, USA	Psychoanalysis	RI, Int	
Gertrude Caton Thompson	1888	1985	England	Archaeology	JC	
* Alice Ball	1892	1916	USA	Medical Chemistry	Wiki	6
Marietta Blau	1894	1970	Austria, USA	Physics	Noyce 2	
Gerty (Radnitz) Cori	1896	1957	Austria-Hungary, USA	Biochemistry	Noyce 2	
Janaki Ammal	1897	1984	India	Botany	RI, Int	
Iréne Joliet-Curie	1897	1956	France	Physics	Noyce 2	
* Joan Beauchamp Procter	1897	1931	England	Herpetology, Zoology	RI, Int	
* Helen Taussig	1898	1956	USA	Medical research	Noyce 2	
Katherine Burr Blodgett	1898	1979	USA	Chemistry and Physics	JC	
Cecilia Payne-Gaposchkin	1900	1979	England, USA	Astronomy	Noyce 2	
* Barbara McClintock	1902	1992	USA	Genetics, Botany	Noyce 1	1983
Marie Goeppert Mayer	1906	1972	Germany, USA	Mathematics, physics	Noyce 2	1963
Grace Murray Hopper	1906	1992	USA	Mathematics, computer programming	Noyce 1	7
* Rachel Carson	1907	1964	USA	Biology	RI, Int	
* Rita Levi-Montalcini	1909	2012	Italy, USA	Embryology, neurology	Noyce 2	1986

	NAME	BIRTH	DEATH	COUNTRY	FOCUS	DATA SOURCE	Notes or Nobel Prize
*	Dorothy Crowfoot Hodgkin	1910	1994	England	Chemistry, crystallography	Noyce 1	1964
*	Anna Jane Harrison	1912	1998	USA	Organic Chemistry	RI, Int	
	Chien-Shien Wu	1912	1997	China, USA	Nuclear physics	Noyce 1	
*	Mary Leakey	1913	1996	England	Paleoanthropologist	RI, Int	
	Hedy Lamarr	1914	2000	Austria, USA	Inventor, actress	RI, Int	
*	Mamie Phipps Clark	1917	1983	USA	Psychology	RI, Int	
*	Gertrude B. Elion	1918	1999	USA	Drug inventor	Noyce 1	1988
	Katherine Johnson	1918	2020	USA	Mathematics, orbital calculations	Wiki	
*	Jane Cooke Wright	1919	2013	USA	Oncology, chemotherapy	Noyce 2	
*	Rosalind E. Franklin	1920	1958	USA	Medical research	Noyce 2	8
*	Rosalyn Sussman Yalow	1921	2011	USA	Physics, nuclear medicine	Noyce 2	1977
*	Marie M. Daly	1921	2003	USA	Biochemistry	JC	
	Mary Jackson	1921	2005	USA	Engineering	JC	
	Stephanie Kwolek	1923	2014	USA	Chemistry	JC	
	Vera Rubin	1928	2016	USA	Astronomy and Astrophysics	JC	
	Edith Marie Flanigen	1929		USA	Chemistry	RI, int	
*	Tu Youyou	1930		China	MD, Pharmacology chemist	Int	9, 2015
	Annie Easley	1933	2011	USA	Mathematics, Computer Science	RI, Int	
*	Jane Goodall	1934		England	Primatology	RI, Int	
*	Sylvia Earle	1935		USA	Marine Biology, Explorer	RI, Int	
*	Ada R. Yonath	1939		Israel	Chemistry, crystallography	Wiki	2009
	Sau Lan Wu	1941		China, USA	Particle Physics	JC	
*	Patricia Bath	1942	2019	USA	Opthalmology, inventor	RI, Int	
	Katia Kraft	1942	1991	France	Volcanology, Geology	RI, Int	
*	Christiane Nüsslein-Volhard	1942		Germany	Genetics, Embryology	Wiki	1995
	Jocelyn Bell Burnell	1943		Ireland, England	Astrophysics	Wiki	
	Shirley Ann Jackson	1946		USA	Physics	RI, Int	
*	Françoise Barré-Sinoussi	1947		France	Virology	Wiki	2008
*	Linda B. Buck	1947		USA	Olfactory physiology	Int	2004
*	Elizabeth Blackburn	1948		Australia, USA	Biology	Wiki	2009
	Alexa Canady	1950		USA	Pediatric Neurosurgery	JC	
	Sally Ride	1951	2012	USA	Physics, engineering	JC	
*	Frances H. Arnold	1956		USA	Chem Engr, Bioengineering, biochemistry	Wiki	2018
*	Mae Jemison	1956		USA	Physician, Engineer, Astronaut	RI, Int	
*	Carol W. Greider	1961		USA	molecular biology	Wiki	2009
*	May-Britt Moser	1963		Norway	Psychology, neuroscience	Wiki	2014
	Tessy Thomas	1963		India	Aeronautical Science	RI, Int	
*	Jennifer Anne Doudna	1964		USA	Biochemistry, CRISPR editing	Wiki	10, 2020
*	Emmanuelle Charpentier	1968		France	Microbiology, genetics, biochemistry	Wiki	2020
	Maryam Mirzakhani	1977	2017	Iran, USA	Mathematics	Wiki	11

NOTES FOR THE APPENDIX

Data is organized by birth date

*This person focused on life-related work

Sources of data -

> Int - Internet
> JC - Jennifer Calvert, *Science Superstars*, St. Martin's Press, NY, 2021
> Noyce 1 - Pendred E. Noyce, *Magnificent Minds*,
>   Tumblehome Learning, Boston, 2015
> Noyce 2 - *Remarkable Minds*, 2016
>   Other data same as above
> RI - Rachel Ignotofsky, *Women In Science*, Ten Speed Press,
>   Berkeley, 2016
> Wiki - Wikipedia

A year entered in the Note column is the time she won the Nobel Prize.

1. Full name, Marie Geneviéve-Charlotte Thireau d'Arconville
2. Fossil collector
3. Countess of Lovelace
4. Co-discoverer of polonium and radium, Noble Prizes 1903, 1911
5. Considered the greatest female mathematician in history
6. Discovered a treatment for leprosy
7. Rear Admiral in the U.S. Navy
8. Co-discoverer of DNA
9. Discovered a treatment for Malaria
10. The subject of a book, *The Code Breaker*, Walter Isaacson, Simon & Schuster, 2021
11. Winner of the Fields Medal